INFORMATION GOVERNANCE

How to regain control

A Practical Guide

by

Bruno Wildhaber

Daniel Burgwinkel

Jürg Hagmann

Stephan Holländer

Peter Neuenschwander

Daniel Spichty

The Swiss Information Governance Competence Center

www.informationgovernance.ch

ISBN 978-3-9524430-3-3

Table of Contents

Figures / Diagrams / Tables

About this book

We live in a world filled with data that is growing at an exponential rate. This rapid growth poses a daunting challenge for many companies. Even SMEs struggle with an ever increasing deluge of information that overwhelms servers and storage devices. As social media gains popularity, data management has become more difficult and this abundance leads to the question about which is the better alternative: "Should data be saved in company files or to a cloud solution"?

The active, controlled handling of data and information is the goal of "Information Governance". Many businesses feel overwhelmed by the concepts and struggle with its implementation. The Competency Centre Records Management (CCRM) and Wildhaber Consulting have tasked themselves with the goal of helping companies overcome these challenges. This book is based on the 2008 Records Management Guide and the Records Management Competency Centre emerged from the work done on the revision of the Swiss retention law. This book focuses on Information Governance as an interdisciplinary field and is the primary source of best practice in Europe. It is a platform for transferring knowledge and provides solutions and advice for Information Governance vendors and customers.

What does this book not do? By no means do the authors claim this book to be comprehensive or to provide all possible theories that apply to this field. The authors have no interest in teaching scientific disciplines such as information science, information technology or business administration, nor do they wish to criticise the teaching of these disciplines. The authors have avoided dogmatic discussions as these have no place in everyday business. This book does not discuss extravagant, strange, theoretical proposals that would confuse and frustrate companies. Instead, the content presented to the reader is based on practical knowledge and real-life project experience.

I would like to thank my colleagues and co-authors Daniel Burgwinkel, Jürg Hagmann, Daniel Spichty, Stephan Holländer, Peter Neuenschwander and Jürg Stutz for the central support (and ideas). I would also like to thank Hans Bärfuss, Beat Lehmann, Michael Rumpf and others who have been actively involved in this work.

Due to the collaborative nature of this book the authors are mentioned in their respective chapters. More information about the authors and partners can be found at the end of this book and on our website. Special thanks to Peter Hill for the translation.

Zurich, August 2016

Bruno Wildhaber, CIP/CISA/CISM/CGEIT

Entrepreneur with a focus on interdisciplinary Information Governance issues, co-founder of the Competency Centre Records Management, lawyer, IT auditor and pinball player.

www.informationgovernance.ch

1. Introduction

1.1 What is this book about?

Bruno Wildhaber

The challenges that arise from appropriate and up-to-date management of information and data have changed the world of computing altogether. This fact is best shown in the introduction to the second edition of the guide “Records Management (RM)”.

“The company’s management sees, in an age of an information society, a challenge which up to now has been previously unknown. Solutions to earlier obstacles such as business data production, administration and accounting were created with much thought and effort. Modern IT systems are important to all business activities, providing significant support and generate a continuous data stream. This electronic data must be constantly monitored, evaluated, distributed, redistributed, checked for quality, corrected, and archived until it is no longer useful and then destroyed. Because of this, data administration is a part of many internal corporate functions; from top management to personnel management, to the IT department. Other stakeholders – investors, creditors, business partners, and government agencies – are keen to know how corporate data is managed.”

What has changed in records management since 2007? The most important development in the field of information processing is the change in perception of the IT department. The involvement of users in the management of information has moved the IT department to the background. The use of numerous Apps and cloud services has removed the need for laborious web-searches and physical visits to the IT department, allowing users to obtain IT services directly from the cloud. But what are the consequences for corporate governance when there is so much freedom?

Corporate governance is certainly not simple. The established bodies and parties that have formally defined rules for governance processes are being constantly questioned and undermined. This confusion regarding the ultimate use of data and information leads to regulatory pressure in many areas of business activity. Excluding the financial industry, new regulations demand rapid implementation and quick results from many companies. Often these regulations relate to data collection. Even small businesses that may have a minor international presence must be cautious and abide by these regulations.

In several areas, legislation places demands on data storage and archiving in order to ensure a minimum standard for the detection of relevant facts and events for Information Governance (IG). Often additional technical and non-technical requirements must be considered. Since the invention of "Records Management", companies can now designate, specify, and manage relevant data in a precise manner. Organisations must keep an increasingly vigilant watch on data that is not subject to retention requirements and possibly not even stored within the company. This raises many questions: Who is responsible for the data on an employee's smartphone? Who ensures that strategic data is available at any time in the cloud, even when the service has been switched off?

IT IS NECESSARY FOR COMPANIES TO MOVE AWAY FROM THE CONCEPT OF A FULLY CONTROLLED "SYSTEM OF RECORDS" AS THIS CONCEPT IS FROM AN ERA OF CARBON COPYING AND CAN NO LONGER BE APPLIED TODAY!

This book therefore introduces new approaches to finding solutions, methods, and concepts that will help companies overcome these challenges.

1.2 The Information Governance Platform

Bruno Wildhaber

1.2.1 The Book – the eBook – the Community

The practical guide of the second edition has been expanded to be the core of a three-part platform composed of the following components:

1. The printed book (practical guide)
2. The eBook (available on Amazon)
3. The community website: www.informationgovernance.ch.

The printed book was created in response to the demand for an easy-to-use eBook. The printed book is intended to serve primarily as a reference and thus remains static while the eBook remains adaptable to current and future circumstances. The guide features case studies and content describing various approaches of responding to the challenges of IG and the implementation of solutions.

The community website was established in order to promote exchanges between stakeholders and to provide a platform that goes beyond a book of theoretical knowledge. It is the aim of the authors to convey the contents of this book in a manner that allows practice and further development. This is done in the hope that this book will become a foundation for the next edition of the guide. The community website includes a discussion platform, content offerings, whitepapers, product information, and latest news on current topics.

1.2.2 The Practical Guide as a Book and eBook

This guide aims to assist with the following problem areas:

- What is meant by modern "Information Governance"? Which components and technical domains are encompassed by this term?
- What are the effects of recent developments in IG on the company's organisation
- What new laws regulate the use of electronic corporate data?
- How can the requirements for corporate governance in the field of maintenance and preservation of business records and documentation be fulfilled?
- What are the industry-specific archiving rules?
- Which documents are companies obliged to preserve?

- Should storage media refresh itself?
- Which emails are to be archived?
- What to consider when conducting business online?
- How does electronic communication affect the auditing process?
- How is data protection guaranteed?
- How important are certifications?
- How should businesses respond when authorities make information requests?
- How should companies implement records management?

This book is a guide for understanding the legal framework as well as an explanation of legally-compliant corporate policies and their implementation. Here the material has been presented so that it applies equally to the management of small and medium enterprises, legal departments of large companies, legal and tax advisors, auditors and IT departments as well as the developers of archiving solutions in regards to the establishment and operation of systems for the collection, use, provision, and storage of electronic business documents.

This is ground breaking work; while the emphasis in the "Records Management" guide was placed on legal issues, this book focuses on implementation processes following Information Governance guidelines and presenting as many solutions as possible. Where no substantive changes have been made, the 2nd edition of the practical guide Records Management should be referred to.

Most books that deal with legal issues highlight problems that arise from regulatory bodies. It is necessary to leave these worn-out paths and provide the reader with the ability to derive their own solutions based on practical examples. For this reason, various practical cases are referenced in this book. Although not all of these projects were successful, experience was gained and therefore a list of suggestions has been compiled for handling such projects successfully in the future.

This book begins with the current challenges of Information Governance and follows with a description of the most important methods to be performed during the implementation phase. For the first time we have developed our own method; the MARIO®[1] trademark of Wildhaber Consulting, Zurich method. This method synthesises the known methods and models and presents them in a business context. By using this method, solutions are formed "top-down" and are actionable from the outset. In addition to these methods, the legal bases that are applicable to both Swiss and international scenarios are discussed. The last chapter focuses on the implementation and application of the methods shown in chapter 2.

In this publication, the terms "company" and "organisation" are used interchangeably. Information Governance is an overarching issue that has importance in both private enterprises and public administration. Therefore, we only refer to one of the mentioned target groups, if this is necessary for legal or technical reasons.

1.2.3 The Community Website: www.informationgovernance.ch

The community website is designed to offer current information to supplement the published guidelines. Using this website, manufacturers and suppliers of services are able to contact each other and access relevant publications. During the compilation of this book, much material could not be used, this information will, however, be published on the community website in the near future. Our website is available in Engish and German, includes a blog in both langiages and we also publish a newsletter.

1.2.4 The companies and parties involved

This guide and the community serve as an information hub for suppliers and clients about Information Governance. Expanding on the last edition, we have deliberately used case studies to show a variety of problems and how to find their solutions. The increasingly complex challenges mean that it is not enough – even for simple problems – to buy an off-the-shelf solution. On the one hand this is annoying, but on the other hand, it is necessary for the correct handling of information. Only sufficient information about market participants and an accurate analysis of the users' needs can lead to a satisfactory solution. The cases depicted in the book are presented in an effort to show case-specific solutions to companies as well as customers.

1.3 Who controls the information?

Bruno Wildhaber

1.3.1 Information usage today

Assumption (Premise) for this book:
We are convinced that a company should control the use of its data and information.

From a business perspective, this means that while it is possible to use data for the purpose of generating immediate earnings, this is only possible for as long as a company complies with the legal data requirements. The latter refers primarily to the fulfilment of statutory regulations in connection to data management. Many of the activities presented here arise in response to regulatory requirements. It should not be forgotten that a private enterprise must always work to satisfy its stakeholders. The balance between the economic aspirations of the company and its compliance to legal obligations must ultimately generate profit.

Regardless of how strongly a company is driven by regulatory requirements, its primary focus should be to identify its data as a production factor and actively work with it. In recent years, new areas of activity have developed which deal with the processing of data inside and outside the company. This topic pertains to the subject of BI (Business Intelligence), which analyses the best ways a company's internal data can be accessed and evaluated. These mechanisms can also be used for customers in an "e-shop". Well-known examples of BI in e-shops include personalised advertisements based on the visitor's search history on the website and "Big Data" where businesses are using large amounts of data to provide intelligence for the company. Today, companies have the opportunity to merge internal and external data pertaining to the behaviour of customers and draw conclusions. For example, by asking a customer, on average, how far and what state of roads he/she travels every day, a car salesman can create a customer profile which will then allow him to sell the customer the optimal car tailored to the customer's needs.

It is now necessary to say good-bye to ubiquitous data control. The old approach of Records Management, which called for just that, in the authors' opinion, must be rendered obsolete. Very few companies are currently able to examine, clean, and track 60-70% of their data. This means that an 80/20 solution is wishful thinking and not feasible with today's tools. Subsequent implementations repeatedly produce the same results. It is essential to refrain from aiming to achieve 100% success in one well-controlled and small working environment while chaos reigns in the rest of the company.

It should not be the purpose nor can it be considered a pilot project representing the situation across the organisation. It is best to start with a minimum set of defined conditions than to adopt a "top down" approach to initiatives that try to control a wide variety of conditions from the start. When minimum requirements are spoken of, they are really meant that way. An analogy from road transport is that we know on which side of the road to travel and that there are traffic rules and we know to focus on the most important ones ("Red means stop"). In the world of Information Governance there is a company-wide specification that sets out the ground rules (e.g. backups are not to an archive) that identify the responsible parties and the applicable actions and sanctions.

1.3.2 The Data Deluge

The handling of information is a major challenge for many organisations today. With new media and ubiquitous digitization, the flood of data continues to grow at a rate never seen before. Further, companies, employees and customers must deal with the growing volumes of information in both business and private life. Companies must approach the issue of information management proactively in order to keep up with the data surge and to avoid unnecessary risks.

These problems include but are not limited to:

- Data volumes continue to increase ("Digital Landfill") but deletion of data is almost impossible as usually it is not known where data is located or whether copies exist.
- Unmanageable data silos continue to multiply. Every App creates its own data stack which cannot be exchanged with others.
- The location of data is never disclosed; increasing the possibility of losing relevant documents.

- Searching for information is becoming more expensive and complicated.
- The ability to provide complete factual information is reduced as information can be falsified and inadequate.
- The accuracy of information cannot be guaranteed.
- Legal requirements cannot be met, thereby exposing the company to massive risks.
- When litigations occur companies must yield to the immense costs caused by documents being manually worked through several times.
- Management and employees are losing confidence in the quality of information processing, IT, and the management of information entrusted to organisational units such as health care providers.
- Operating costs increase as the search for information is more time consuming
- Departments, which are responsible for IM, lose credibility because they cannot meet the growing information needs. Financially independent customers look for external solutions.

1.3.3 Data Anarchy?

The discussions about data and its development in recent years raise two main issues - data protection and privacy. The NSA/Snowden scandal has shown that today's intelligence agencies are equipped and willing to systematically gather and compile large amounts of data, and have done so successfully for at least 20 years, while companies today still struggle.

These developments show that data is becoming more and more important. Today many third parties are interested in personal data. Up until a few years ago cyber-crime was not a credible threat and posed little significant risk. In the past stolen data could not be used for significant financial gain and therefore there was little incentive compared to the risks involved. This has now changed and today cyber-crime has escalated as a result of government and criminal organisations hiring hackers to collect personal information. In the following chapters, we will discuss some of the interesting points concerning data security.

It is very apparent from observing discussions on copyright, authorship, IT industry, and from various interest groups that the value of data continues to increase rapidly. Despite the age of this debate, solutions still appear to be out of reach. Ancient businesses models meet new technologies. Policies tend to apply the latest developments to old models, consequently often result in failure. The helpless executive can only watch with disdain as these projects fail. In a few years it is expected that copyright will appear as in issue in a business context and form a permanent point of contention. The open-source movement demands that former traditional licensing models be replaced by more appropriate commercial alternatives. Until this is completed, all stakeholders will have to come to terms with the uncomfortable challenges that data creates.

Our forecast: Organisations will have to prove the origin of their data. This is a classic documentation problem. Imagine there is an exemplary company with established retention requirements, which have recognised the basic principle of accountability. This company would do well to apply the principles of information management to all its data and to consider what rights the company and its employees have to what content.

Consider data on the smartphone of an employee; does it actually belong to the business? Is it the employees who decide which hardware will be used by the enterprise in the future? Can employees claim sovereignty over the data on a smartphone? If the latter is the norm, then the floodgates of data abuse are opened. Even with the most sophisticated security mechanisms, it will not be possible to adequately protect company resources. Of course, this reasoning assumes there will be a need for business secrets in the future, and intangible assets are not available to view online. Information Governance must therefore deal with the question of who owns what data and how to give effect to what is claimed.

1.3.3.1 What remains of privacy?

The current interest in data security and the personal right to privacy is yet to reach a climax. These topics are being discussed widely across all media platforms. The protection of privacy is a fundamental human right. German Chancellor, Angela Merkel's statement "For all of us, the internet is unexplored territory" has some truth. Although people may have been using the Internet for years, the social level of their online activity is still far from mature. In other words, often times, the average internet user's developmental level is similar to that of a ten year old child. This is true even for "digital natives" who, although they have learned much about using the Internet sensibly, often do not put this knowledge into practice.

It can be expected then that in the next few years, data protection rules will become more stringent in many parts of the world (for example the upcoming EU data regulation and the discussions following the end of the "Safe Harbor" agreement in 2016). This trend will lead to operators and owners of databases being required to justify how they use the data they possess and who has access to it at any given time. While this already exists in today's data protection laws, it is not strictly enforced. At an international level it can be expected that the issue of privacy will last for as long as data is used as an economic weapon. Just as good product quality is a major selling point, the high quality of data processing will also become a selling point and serve to eliminate competitors from the data-trade game. Although free-trade zones which lack the usual restrictions on trade will be exploited, more barriers to international traffic will be introduced. The debate regarding the breakdown of Internet jurisdiction and domains is long overdue.

1.4 New Technologies and Changes in User Behaviour

Jürg Hagmann / Dieter Schmutz / Bruno Wildhaber

1.4.1 User Driven IT

Since the advent of combining mobile devices and interactive technologies (e.g. social media), the balance of power in the digital world has shifted fundamentally; away from the organisation and over to the users.

Globalization, the subversive effect of hyperlinks and hierarchy flattening, coupled with an entitlement to empowerment, have enabled users to actively determine which tools are best used for what purpose. Companies which have the potential now realise the process: -> Unleash your employees -> energise your customers -> transform your business.

In 2008 Josh Bernoff, of Forrester, coined the term "groundswell" to mean a social trend in which people use technology to achieve what they want and not what the institution offers. The combination of this trend with new technology and the online economy is a rapidly growing phenomenon. User-driven IT allows smart companies to attract the talents needed to acquire and maintain business. Consequently, a new agreement is needed between the organisation and the user (Bailey).

The reason for the success of user-driven IT is its "openness to use" by devices (BYOD) and networks (BYON). The users decide how they use the tools provided and which use will be considered efficient. This also has an impact in the development of application systems. The traditional SDLA model is still applied, ignoring the strong demand from the user side. In a world of abundant cloud offerings, the user community is no longer willing to accept long development cycles. A paradigm shift is occurring and more and more companies are following this direction.

Enterprise 1.0	Enterprise 2.0
Hierarchical	Lean organization
Complex processes	Simple organizational processes
Bureaucracy	Flexibility
IT driven by technology, no user control	User driven technology
Top-down structures	Distributed
Centralistic	Global teams
Teams in office buildings, designated areas	Blurred boundaries, flexible office spaces
Knowledge is concentrated	Knwoledge is distributed and ubiquitous
IT-Systems are structured and well governed (IT Governance)	Information is a service (N. Carr)
Taxonomy	Folksonomy
Proprietary standards	Open
Well planned	On demand
Time to market; SDLA development	Ad hoc, short development cycles, agile development

1.4.2 Cloud

"Cloud computing" or just "cloud", in all its possible combinations, since 2009, is the popular marketing term for a variety of Internet based IT services throughout the world. In 2009 the US National Institute of Standards and Technology (NIST) defined the term "Cloud Computing" and finalised the definition in September 2011 in NIST Special Publication 800-145. It is this definition that is used by the European Network and Information Security Agency (ENISA).

It is to the merit of NIST, and probably the reason for the durability, this definition identifies the three aspects of characteristics, services, and deployment models, each with clearly distinct traits. Depending on the context (or selling point) organisations often use only individual features for each definition. For a proper expert examination of the Cloud it is well worth reading the NIST definition.

The German Federal Office for Security in Information Technology (BSI) website provides a German translation of the above-mentioned source and formulated its own definition in line with this as follows:

"Cloud Computing contains dynamically tailored pay-per-use IT-service offerings which take place exclusively via defined technical interfaces and protocols. The range of services offered in the context of cloud computing covers the full range of information technology and includes, among other infrastructure (e.g. computing power, memory), platforms and software. "

These services are cumulative; the lowest level comprises the physical infrastructure components (IaaS). Next the cloud providers provision operating systems and corresponding service platforms (PaaS) as patch services, monitoring and possibly offering backup solutions. The third tier, Software-as-a-Service (SaaS), is the provision of specific application systems. The term ASP (Application Service Providing) is sometimes used interchangeably with SaaS and was – in the context of outsourcing – used even before the cloud era. The NIST definition has clarified that cloud computing ventures beyond traditional outsourcing of customer applications in an ASP environment and includes, in particular, a dynamic component and "self-service" management. Many users are short-term and scale their cloud capacity to fulfil current needs and in accordance with pre-agreed terms and conditions.

Clearly cloud computing should play a role in any modern sourcing strategy, if only to establish test systems or sandboxes for prototyping and pilot projects. Cloud services can be quickly established, are easily made available, and can be terminated when no longer needed. This benefits not only large companies or corporations, who make use of cloud in their own and others' data centres (called a "private cloud"), but in particular to medium-sized and very small companies which can benefit from public cloud offerings of IT services with consistent reliability, high availability, and security. Such cloud services are often invaluable to these companies as they are not always able to have their own cloud on their premises due to limited personnel. This view is not shared by all potential users, but applies in the majority of cases.

Which company with 5 – 50 employees can claim that all security updates (security patches) are, at any one time, up to date so that they have a complete security infrastructure with fire protection systems, emergency power supply, firewalls, and a 24 hour monitoring for rapid response? Usually such a standard cannot be maintained by smaller organisations with their in-house IT, for a reasonable cost. Why then are so many companies waiting? The answer is simple and consistent with the findings that are explained in the other chapters of this book. The technical possibilities are enticing but the conceptual, organisational, and legal challenges will not be solved by technology. Good governance and sufficient due diligence is required before going to the cloud. First analyse the worst-case scenario and make satisfactory arrangements with the cloud/sourcing partner regarding:

- How is operation of the service continued if the provider goes bankrupt?
- If his installations are destroyed by a catastrophic event?
- If the supplier is taken over by another company?
- If strict data protection rules are not complied with at all times?
- Are the confidentiality agreements with the staff or the external partner?

A good "Proof of Concept" will demonstrate how the process looks like in detail when data is retrieved from the cloud or is migrated to another provider. This should include ensuring that after leaving the cloud the data remains organised, without missing or misplaced information. Consequently this "coin" has two sides: one with convincing advantages and the other showing major challenges in the field of architectural design and contract specification.

These challenges must be addressed with the appropriate competence. The reality is that the cloud is an important element in IT sourcing. There are many reasons that support the assertion that cloud computing represents a fundamental and permanent change in how IT services are provided, operated, and used.

Just as factories are no longer built on riverbanks, or people no longer need to drive, it is no longer appropriate that every company – small or large – should find it essential to use their own or external server data centres.

The questions one must ask the cloud-sourcing-partners are the same that apply to the company's "on premises" operation. Such questions pertain to:

- How capacity adjustment (scaling) is performed and the lifecycle of the hardware, operating system, and applications are managed.
- What happens in the case of fire or water damage?
- What if data is stolen by an employee or in a hacker attack?
- What if the software supplier ceases trading?

You will then understand whether sourcing via the cloud represents a viable alternative. This is especially true when geographical and legal territory provide advantageous conditions.

1.4.3 Appification

Apps on a smartphone are very practical and are now an indispensable part of the business world. Company-specific applications are as available, flexible and user-friendly as any other consumer app. Mobile devices can be easily connected and integrated to the IT systems of the company. Conventional methods of operational application deployment are no longer effective in the new user-driven (user-centric) IT model. IT management must find a way to manage new technologies and to provide services without increasing the operational costs or the complexity of administration. The number of users who expect enterprise software to take on the characteristics of an app will increase significantly. Software manufacturers should therefore provide licensing, activation, and select deployment models that meet the needs of this target group. But doing so presents some challenges for business units and manufactures. The control of software cycles including the creation of controlling policies (change one of these controls to regulate, I don't know which one should be changed), practices and guidance is critical, but the key to counteracting unbridled proliferation of apps is installing preventative measures. The development, management, and maintenance of a variety of new unconventional license models will take time, resources, and money – as will the recording of the back-office privileges of users.

1.4.4 The Change of IT

The developments illustrated here show that the role of the typical IT department has either already moved on or will do so in the coming years. It has been known for at least 10 years, since the article by Carr[XXXX] "IT does not matter" that the golden age of the IT department as it was then, has come to an end. Today there is an enormous potential for tension between traditional IT and the representatives of a generation that primarily performs data processing through apps. Even with the current trends that contribute to the industrialization of IT, this potential for conflict cannot be easily resolved. Industrialization means rigid structuring of processes and predetermined performance expectations; a development that would preclude the current trend of data usage diametrically. Most of the classical transaction systems, as we know them today, have basic features that were developed in the seventies. One has to keep in mind that at that time, workers clocked in and out with punch cards. Data was sequential, read in large decks, and processed by a central computer. While these basic principles are still valid, today's computing power enables completely different applications and usage patterns.

The basic principles of Records Management were developed in the early IT-age. The counting of punch cards and the generation of checksums are control mechanisms that have been taught to IT auditors for decades. If modern information systems are developed using the same methods, it is no wonder that the number of wayward IT projects has not decreased in recent years. This would be the equivalent of developing Formula 1 racing cars using the design of steam engines.

Now an extra dimension is added. Data can no longer be held under one roof, but must be stored at different locations and be readily accessible. This does not necessarily simplify the process. The aspect of data control was only considered marginally. Again the question arises of whether or not the company knows about the organisation of its data and if it can be queried at any time – a typical IM and IG question.

If IT has lost sovereignty over the business' data, it is essential that the business now takes responsibility for its data. But this is the very beginning of the end of the story; a user who is aware of the responsibility of handling corporate data deserves praise from the employer. Without the corresponding sense of responsibility, all measures that we describe in the context of Information Governance will eventually fail.

1.5 Business Challenges

Bruno Wildhaber

We have seen that the handling of information is not a matter to be left to chance, but instead must be addressed in an entrepreneurial manner. Irrespective of the different problems for the entrepreneur, the following basic requirements pose challenges to management:

- Enable the optimal use of information.
- The earliest possible detection of information including determining the information's significance (i.e. taxonomy) to the enterprise.
- The prevention of unnecessary data storage, the deletion of redundant data, and the weeding out irrelevant data.
- Finding data and information at any time.
- Guaranteeing business orientation and ensuring the traceability of transactions.
- Guaranteeing security and privacy at all times.
- Coordinating activities of various disciplines (technology, IT, organisation, business, law, etc.) and direct the strategic contribution over the long term.
- Giving the business a responsible position and encourage coordination with IT.
- Promoting awareness of the importance of managing information at all levels.
- The quantification of risks in connection with data management systems.
- Relaying important resource information to management and describing the need for action.
- Initiating concerted actions that lead to a structured and planned approach.

2 Basics

2.1 Governance of the Organisation

Bruno Wildhaber

2.1.1 Corporate Governance

Corporate governance has been shaped by the definition and understanding of the OECD. This model, which mainly contains a strong focus on control aspects, only proves worthy if there is a proactive implementation and the board is actively involved. It is understood that Corporate Governance, as the holistic management of a company at the highest level by its governing body (board), must determine, direct, implement, and monitor good governance. Corporate governance refers to all facets of business management. The concept of creative governance is characterised by the model of the "New Corporate Governance" developed at the Institute for leadership of the university in St. Gallen headed by Professor Dr. Hilb (Hilb, 2013). Prof. Hilb addresses the urgent need for leadership among the board of directors (quote "From the supervisory to the formative board"). These general principles are decisive for entrepreneurial activity and run through and at all management levels.

The central attributes of this model are:

1. The continuous control of all success factors at the board level
2. The integrated and holistic approach to all aspects of corporate oversight at board level
3. Understanding the strategic corporate design as a key board function instead of a purely supervisory role, and
4. The situational and targeted adaptation of corporate governance to the individual context of an affected company.

Like a thread through the entire governance model, the four basic principles Hilb developed are similar to the usual KISS factors that are derived in accordance with the above explanation as follows:

K: Keep it controlled (evaluation unit): COMMAND & CONTROL
I: Keep it integrated (board / management dimension): COMMUNICATE AND EXECUTE INTEGRATIVE
S: Keep it strategic (design dimension): FOLLOW THE STRATEGY AND FOCUS ON LONG-TERM OBJECTIVES
S: Keep it situational (context dimension): ACT SITUATIONAL WITHOUT SACRIFICING STRATEGY

Governance activities must be evaluated using the following five measurement criteria:

1. **Increase the company's value** and support company development,
2. **Value added** to and support for all core processes of the value chain,
3. **Controlled** treatment of risks
4. Optimal use of resources and
5. **Continuous review and optimization** of the information system with regard to these criteria.

Corporate governance refers to the responsibility of the Executive Board, the management, and the entrepreneurs or owners who must achieve the objectives mentioned above. Content means that the management structures, organisational structures, and the necessary processes to implement these goals need to be established. The main stakeholders here are the staff, the owners (shareholders), the environment (external stakeholders), and the customer.

But how is Information Governance to be understood in this context?

From the perspective of employers and stakeholders, information is provided as a resource to implement business strategies of varying relevance. The focus, therefore, is the question of how much information can be used as a value-adding factor for the company and how much should processing of information be reduced for the proper handling of risks.

First, the entrepreneur or management should ask the question; what is the role of information as a resource in their organisation?

2.1.2 The Importance of Information in the Company: the GDAS-Model

The board must understand and immediately address important questions regarding the processing of information. How far this commitment will go depends directly and exclusively on the importance and role of information processing within the company.

Information processing – or technology, organisational structures, hardware, and software – must be treated as a resource for strategic management. Each board member should be aware of the importance of information as a resource. This requires an examination of the role of information processing in the company and the documented accountability of the board. It is not enough to leave these tasks to management at the strategic or normative levels. An active debate on the issue should be placed on the agenda of the board.

Information processing within the company can be positioned in various ways. A positioning model has been developed that serves as a guide for the correct placement of information processing.

The GDAS-model illustrates how information processing should develop within the company:

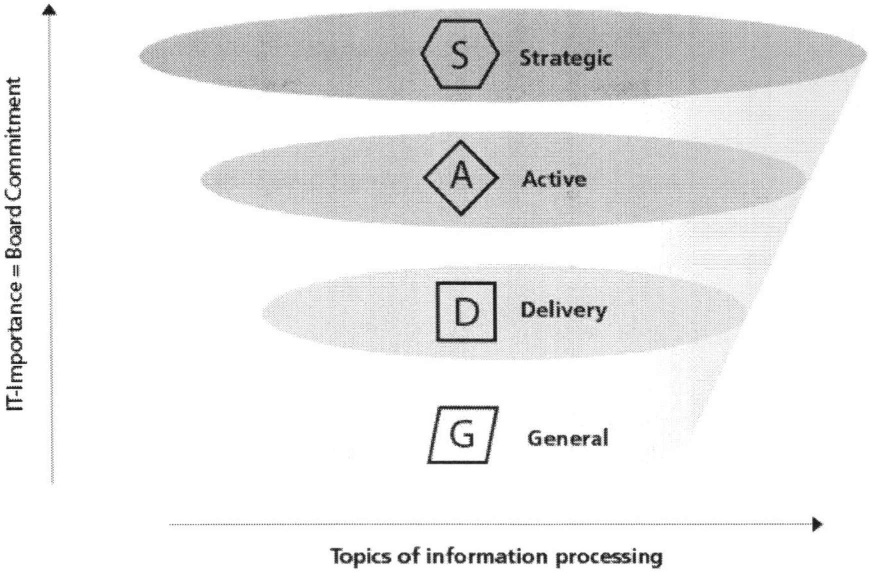

Fig. 1: GDAS Model

In summary, the GLAS-model is as follows In-depth information at Bienert / Wildhaber, sect 2.4.1

DELIVERY	STRATEGIC
Information/IT as a resource/ infrastructure with partial importance in certain business areas **As a rule, purely supportive.** **Generally supports individual productivity processes, and the core business processes can be handled without IT (substitutable); although the operating costs will increase sharply.** **In case of failure, support can be dispensed from IT readily within several days. With core processes the maximum downtime will be two days. Failure is not threatening.** **Typical applications**	The company provides information processing as a core service (information management is the primary focus of IT) This is the most important production factor (implies data and information are intangible assets) and is vital for both production and support; omnipresent. IT supports the company's results; Cash flow is directly dependent on IT services. IT also has a supporting function (e.g. Internet, office automation) and serves as a key infrastructure component. Networked organisation, mostly international communications. Companies cannot provide services without IT.

DELIVERY	STRATEGIC
• **Accounting** • **Personnel administration** • **Control of simple production** **Typical IT Budget-spending:** **2-5%**	Failures < 1 days have serious consequences and are almost impossible to compensate.
Examples: - **Manufacturing Industry** - **Chemical (industrial)** - **Automotive** - **Management** **Distribution:** **In service companies today the minority < 25%**	Examples: - IT companies - IT service provider (clearing houses, etc.) - Banking (E-banking) - E-Government - Telecommunications - And other E-services Typical IT Budget Spending: 20 – 40 %
GENERAL	ACTIVE
Information/ IT as a resource/ infrastructure of minor significance. **Purely supportive.** **Supports any development or execution of core competencies. In case of failure can be waived without further repercussions for several days.** **Typical applications:** - **Accounting** - **Personnel Administration** **Typical IT budget spending:** **<2%** **Examples:** **Companies in the primary sector: agriculture, artisans, SMEs.** **Distribution:** **In service companies today the minority <25%**	Information/ IT as a resource/ infrastructure with significant importance in the central business areas Supports the core processes of the company and has a significant share of added value. Cash flow is dependent on at least 50 percent of IT. IT also has a supporting function (e.g. Internet, office automation) and serves as a key infrastructure component. A failure <2 days may have significant impact on the operations result. The loss can pose a long-term threat to their {the company's} existence. Typical applications: Banks Companies with a high degree of automation Control of complex systems Typical IT Budget Spending: 10 – 20% Examples: -banks

DELIVERY	STRATEGIC
	-Financial Services -Pharmaceuticals - management - insurance Distribution: In service companies today the majority.

2.1.3 The management context: The conformance-performance dilemma (CONFPERF-chart)

Entrepreneurial activity is influenced by many different factors. All decision-making relies on the balance between optimization of the business and compliance with internal and external rules. In other words, "Corporate governance is the ability to deal constructively with conflicts of objectives and interests" (Prof. R. H. Dubs). But how can these aspects be balanced? What decisions must be made and for what price? In what context is this information used?

- The PERFORMANCE – CONFORMANCE model shows the co-dependency of the outcomes to be "value-oriented" (performance) and "adhering to rules, obligations and commitments" (conformance). It will be used to visualise the information driven initiatives and projects.

Example: Management can build new business models only if they comply with rules set by the normative level (typically the board). The trade-off between income and expenses, arising from the observance of regulations, is a typical decision-balancing act. The security cost (access control and other risk based measures) must be proportional to the expected financial gains.

Fig. 2: Conformance / Performance

The diagram shows two axes with CONFORMANCE below the vertical axis and PERFORMANCE above. Each management decision moves along this axis. Normally strategic initiatives begin and settle on this axis. This observation applies to static or one-time decisions and also to everyday decisions that management must make. Many decisions are made in this manner. For example:

- Must this investment be made because of regulatory pressure?
- If I invest in this business will I receive direct profits or benefits from it?

If only this axis existed, informed decisions would be very hard to make.
Many decisions, however, are located in no man's land, that is, there are decisions that are at first glance not obviously close to either extreme. In order to visualise this, the horizontal axis is used. On this axis, to the left lies costs and to the right the value generated. Hence we have a quantitative representation – usually of a monetary nature. Here a system has been created on which it is possible to observe the long-term impact of a particular business decision. Example: A company developing a new product might be planning on increasing its market share. Using this business case in conjunction with the infographic, it is possible to see this example move into the profit quadrant. Caution is necessary as value orientation directly impacts the financial results. The new product has to have an increased profit

goal. This involves increasing the company's value by achieving a better economic result (bottom line), which does not arise through financial engineering, but rather through real business growth.

The quadrants and their meaning will become clearer once defensive and progressive strategies have been addressed. Progressive strategies are always located in the top right corner while defensive strategies are found in the bottom left (the illustration includes the funding of a project in "costs". Focusing on costs entails a more defensive attitude towards new initiatives. The upper left quadrant is therefore dedicated to value achieving considering costs. Existing products that improve or simplify manufacturing processes reduce cost.

In the lower right quadrant lies risk management where an enterprise is CONFORMANCE oriented but also hopes to achieve value with their project. Business results that can be predetermined through a well-controlled method are more likely to provide a competitive advantage. This advantage may, for example, allow companies to follow legal requirements as efficiently as possible. As a situational example, one might take the cold chain that is required by a retailer when delivering food ("A cold chain is a temperature-controlled supply chain. An unbroken cold chain is an uninterrupted series of storage and distribution activities which maintain a given temperature range"; Source: Wikipedia). Not every retailer is able to ensure this. Can a supplier procure the necessary funds to deliver the product to the consumer? By doing so then he can open up a new market that was previously closed to him. To achieve this, he must not only have the means of delivery, but also a comprehensive product control system and the drive to continuously monitor logistic activities.

The bottom left quadrant has, so far, been neglected. But, it is of significant importance. This area is the quadrant in which the majority of activities settle once processed by better Information Governance.

Can this illustration really help in daily project life? Most definitely, this will be seen in chapter 2.1.4 when it is demonstrated that the decision on an IM strategy leads to the adoption of a set of basic assumptions and rules that represent a "constitution" and serves as the basis for all approved projects. A project, which finds itself in the compliance quadrant, cannot be moved suddenly to the value corner! It seems obvious, but such action is often attempted when management changes or projects must suddenly have a ROI.

A compliance project does not generate a cash cow just as a tractor does not magically change into a Formula 1 vehicle.

As already mentioned, Information Governance issues tend to lie within the lower left quadrant. "Archiving" is an example that demonstrates this well. All companies have archived documents over the years. With the introduction of IT, the consciousness and practice of archiving electronic data grew – be it for the establishment of a historical archive, to follow regulations or to prepare for cases of unjustified claims. With the introduction of records, a new profession and discipline developed. The "Record Manager" was born; the position responsible for the controlled handling of "Records".

As mentioned, most companies were originally driven by compliance. Since compliance is a defensive topic, any investment with this strategic focus is always risk-oriented. While records management is concerned exclusively with the topic of conformity, IM goes much further. It is imperative that IM includes value-added components and does not retreat into a position of compliance. One caveat must be mentioned; data management and the proper handling of information is a fundamental basis for achieving benefits. If a company wishes to introduce a new business process or launch a new product, information becomes an increasingly important factor in decision making. For example, the active maintenance of data quality is not only a compliance measure it also has a direct impact on all other quadrants.

While quality aspects will always lead to a strategic advantage, the same might be true for regulatory, audit, and security considerations.
The Information Governance model presented here will address these aspects.

Benefits of the CONFORMANCE – PERFORMANCE model

1. The model shows the long-term alignment of various initiatives and can be used for a variety of projects.
2. The visualization makes it possible to, at any time, reproduce the orientation of a project and communicate the project motivation and objectives.
3. It promotes an understanding of business context and the chosen strategies
4. It highlights imbalances in strategic implementation and helps in correcting the product / project portfolio flaws.
5. It can be used at all levels due to its convincing simplicity.
6. It can be used to define goals and metrics.

2.1.4 IT-Governance

The figure below shows:

- the levels of governance
- the position of information (value factor), and
- IT (executive element, including values, methods, and objects).

Fig. 3: IT and Information Governance

This forms the cornerstone of the model explained below for Information and IT-governance:

- Information / IT governance must correspond to the form and extent of the company's individual circumstances.
    - Depending on the importance of information as a success factor, Information Governance either plays a strong or submissive role.

    - IT Governance promotes transparency in decision-making processes and the benefits information produces for the business.
- Information / IT governance must be understood as a design element of strategic management.
    - Information is a critical foundation for the required process quality and is closely linked to its continuous improvement.
    - Business models for IT are of a more infrastructural character and are threatened today by existential failure.
    - IT represents a significant cost and risk factor that must be understood and controlled directly at a board level.
- Information / IT governance is interlocked with the operational implementation level and the management of IT projects and systems.
    - Large IT projects within the IT sector involve high risks for multiple and significant violations of schedule and budget.
    - The necessary understanding of IT in the language and experience of the board can only be achieved through the higher presence of the board and the pressure generated thereby to the operating units to communicate with the normative organs (follow 'Nose in - Hands out' principle).

- Information / IT governance must include a framework and requirement for stringent key performance indicator systems of IT providing a current and highly condensed look at performance and cost of IT.
    - Performance indicator systems are a new field for IT and therefore require special attention.
    - Indicators are the most efficient operating method of performance measurement for IT infrastructure.
    - Performance and cost may only be measured if the scope of services provided is measurable.
    - Control systems also apply to the control of IT governance itself, whose development depends on permanent monitoring whether they serve the growth of the capabilities of the company or not.

Keeping these considerations in mind, we have developed the following IT governance model:

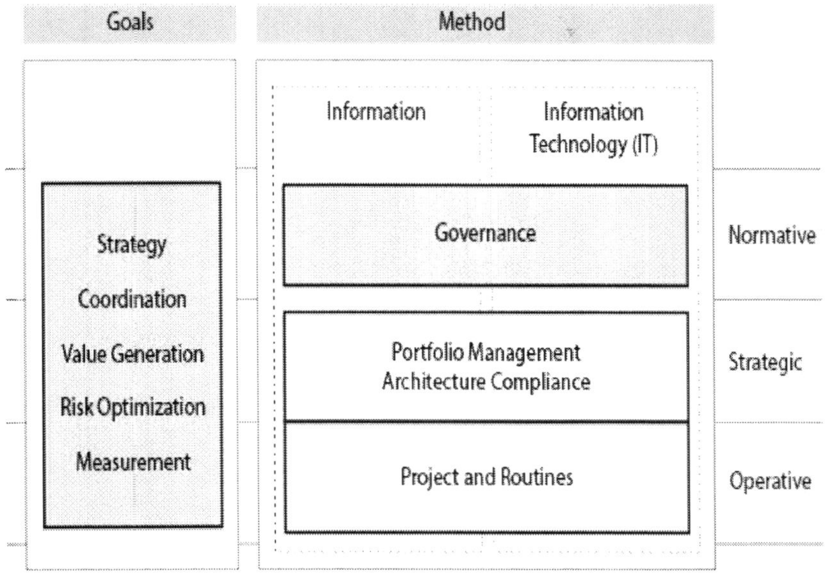

Fig. 4: Model of IT Governance

From the authors' point of view, architecture and (project) portfolio management are the key elements necessary to achieve manageable governance. These elements need to be coupled with measurements and controls. In addition, routines and escalation procedures must be established and practiced repeatedly. As with all governance issues, usually far too much importance are given to preventive aspects resulting in the neglecting of (criminal) monitoring. For further information about IT governance and the implementation of a comprehensive IT governance framework, it is recommend the COBIT™ framework and its available materials are consulted and followed.

2.1.5 Distinguishing between Information and IT governance

IT governance classically deals with all aspects of information processing, but not primarily with the business value of IT or the value of information in the organisation. Here, IT governance means, above all, the control of information processing methods, components, and resources. In other words, if IT is performed in accordance with the applicable rules and procedures and the cost of performance is affordable, success is most likely to follow? Are these procedures and controls sufficient and allow for the achievement of set goals?

This understanding continues to characterise the practice of IT governance, although the relevant organisations, especially ISACA, are desperately trying to change this. ISACA was formerly known as the IT Auditors Association (USA) and is still dominated by members of this profession. The organisation often acts defensively, and primarily focuses on risk aspects. COBIT™ (ISACA, 2013) is an IT governance and management framework that was developed by ISACA and regarded as a reference model for IT governance. Unfortunately COBIT presently has such an unmanageable complexity that it is difficult to apply to business. As a result, IT governance is usually perceived from a control perspective and less from that of strategic management, or as a value-adding factor. This guide strongly advocates the use of IT governance methods, but is aware that the variety of available procedures for organisations is often a hindrance. The authors believe that these methods should mainly be applied during the implementation process and the proper operation of information technology solutions to IT governance issues. Today, this primarily relates to sourcing issues where IT governance plays a very important role. Limited application in special fields is to be expected if an IT governance framework is only just being introduced. Companies must be sure to remember that implementing such a framework is an ongoing task that for many has just begun. Without clear objectives, an IT governance initiative should not be launched.

2.1.6 Risk Management & due Diligence

According to the principles of corporate governance, a board must establish an internal control system (ICS). In many countries Statutory Auditors are obliged to examine and confirm the existence of the ICS in their audit report. In addition, it is required that companies operate a risk management method that allows the assessment of the state of the risks in the enterprise. Changes in risks should always be transparent. The implementation of this risk assessment forms part of the audit of the annual financial statements.

The risks in relation to information include, in particular, loss, alteration, disclosure to unauthorised parties, improper use, and the non-existence or loss of quality of evidence of the existing information. The growth of these requirements is increasing the diversity of special legal regulations that conventional storage systems must address.

The risk management system is independent of the use of certain technologies or processes. Where or how much effort is exerted depends essentially on the nature of business operations and experience. If it is an issue that is completely new for the company, one must first carry out a comprehensive risk analysis.

Risk management entails recording identified risks with various measures of a technical, organisational, personnel, and financial nature but excludes, reduces, or deliberately does not take any unnecessary entrepreneurial risks. The residual risks must also be identified and listed. This overview must be presented to decision-makers in the company. The decision about what actions or which causes of residual risks should be taken into account is the sole responsibility of company management.

In accordance with the principles of governance it can be seen that the nature and extent of the measures used to conduct due diligence in establishing a risk management system for the company's activities and the importance of each data category contribute significantly to the company's success.

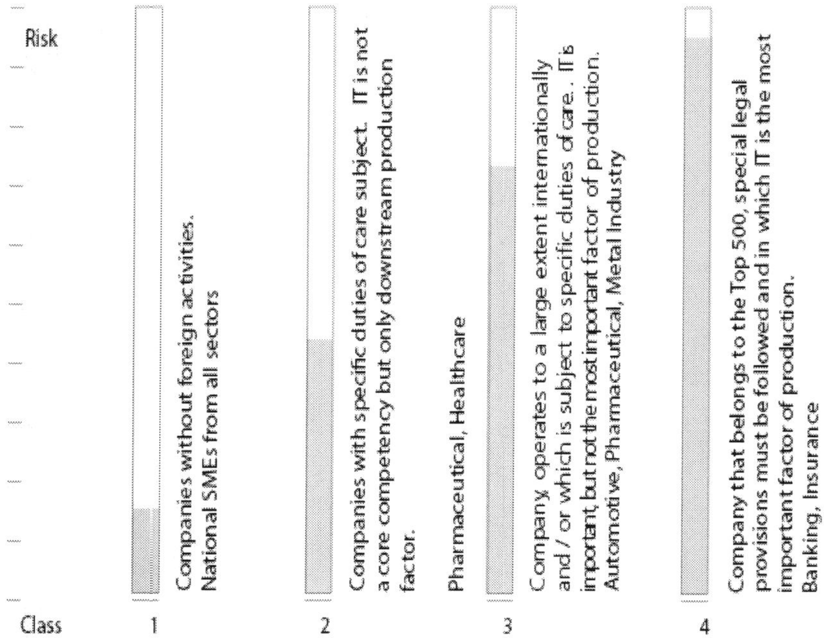

Fig. 5: Risk classes

The nature of the business, the involvement of information as well as regulatory pressure defines the general risk positioning of the organisation. Figure 5 shows that companies which do operate with information processing at their core must put more effort into risk management than a traditional manufacturing company.

In many companies, however, no uniform due diligence assessment (risk level) can be made. In many enterprises, a very high level of care is only required for select processes. For example, a food company must meet the highest standard in food production through the implementation of production processes that maximise production as well as quality control. However such high standards are not necessary for the accounting function of this operation. Consequently the question arises as to how one should deal with such a situation. In the past, most errors committed during implementation occurred while seeking security clearance of the highest level. This level was equally applied to all systems. This approach failed as a result of the high costs and impractical nature of the security measures in simpler processes.

Within this general categorization there can be further granularity. Figure 6 below shows concrete implementation in accordance with the defined classes. A class 4 falls in the range of the 80/20 ratio. This means that an increase in the level of care of a class 4 risk topic will result in a disproportionate use of resources. In this area, it is ideal if a company proceeds purposefully and takes appropriate precautions when approaching identified risks. This approach ensures an optimum distribution of risk and value creation.

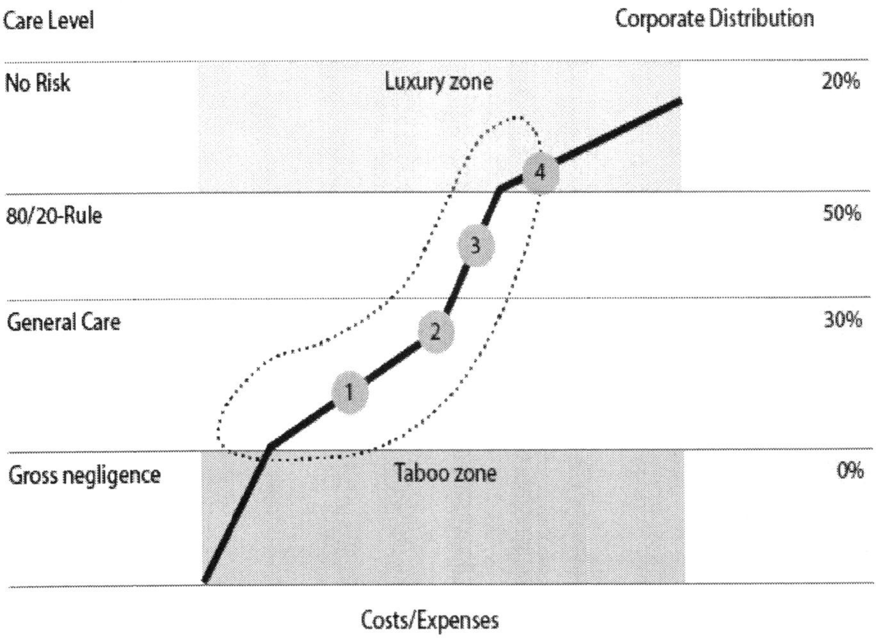

Fig. 6: Risk banana

It should be noted that many decisions must be made regarding the structure of a risk management system and the applicable safeguards outside the generally circumscribed legal retention requirements. It is therefore conceivable that a company will choose, generally or for a specific field of activity, to establish a comprehensive risk management system. Other organisations might decide to fulfil the minimum standard only. This example shows that acting on circumscribed areas and standard requirements may not always lead to an appropriate solution. Rather, decision-makers must make a judgement call.

Example: Basic questions regarding the objective, subject, nature, and extent of a records management program as specified in the standard ISO 15489 (see Glossary) must be resolved before such a project can be started.

There are no hard rules about which books, data, documents, correspondence, etc. need to be created and stored. Direct and clear answers to the questions of what is kept and what is not, must not be asked until an analysis has been carried out regarding the entirety of an enterprise's stored and continuously generated data and documents and the management of risk has been considered. Keeping everything that falls within the broad circumscribed legal retention requirements does not necessarily make economic sense.

These cases have to be identified and a clear decision made regarding their retention. From the perspective of efficiency, the approach to keep "as much as possible" (luxury zone) is ruled out. Significant technical, organisation, and legal risks (discovery obligations, privacy requirements) may result when virtually all related documents, including internal notes and e-mails are kept for an undefined period of time.

Targeted destruction is as important as controlled storage. These preliminary questions must be answered before decisions are made to implement possible solutions.

Risk management calls for the establishment of a system that includes the following activities:

- Risk identification
- Risk analysis
- Decisions on counter measures (implementation).

To be added as permanent activities:

- Continuous monitoring / control / so-called gap analysis (i.e. measurement of deviations)
- Risk management (decisions about how to treat individual risks is a task of the board or executive management)

Every risk management system follows similar procedures. Essentially, it is necessary to first ensure that a risk-prone state of affairs is always detected. Thereafter one applies a method which is usually the combination of analysing the actual risks and best-practice based on the available regulations and standards. With the best practice methods defining the basis for correct operation (i.e. a recognised method) it is now possible to take into account due diligence. The specific risk analysis is used to detect increased risks (e.g. introduction of a new archive system).

It should be noted that in the development and implementation of IM / RM systems, one should always proceed from an analysis of business processes and never proceed with the simple adaptation of so-called best practice methods. This is the only way to meet the demands of IT Governance for alignment of IM systems with the needs of business.

The weakness of known risk analysis methods is that they assume that the company knows what data it owns. This assumption is incorrect as shown in the context of the discussion regarding the amount of data and challenges it poses today (chap. 1).

Most organisations are protecting (ROT[1]) data with expensive security measures!

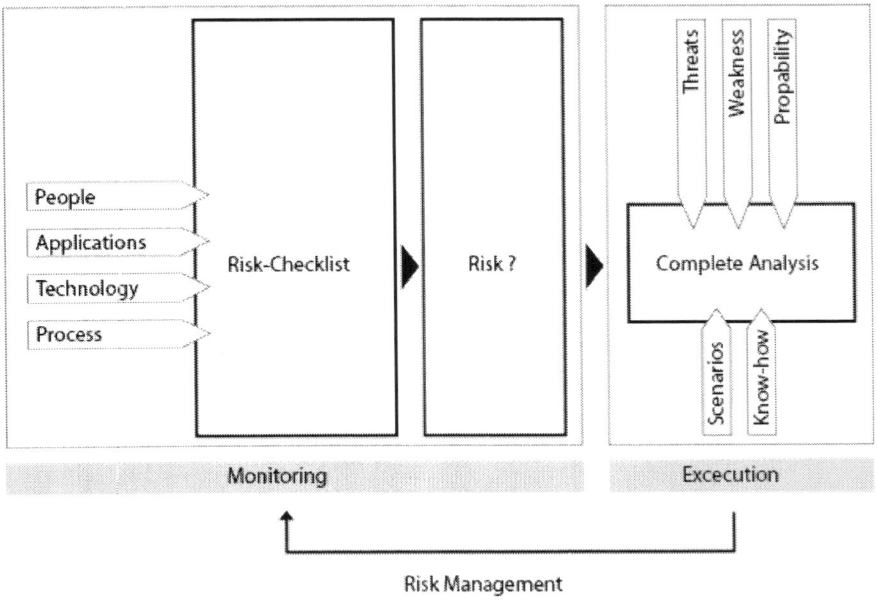

Fig. 7: Risk management method

[1] Redundant, Obsolete or Trivial; according to recent studies approximately 70% of data within the company is either unknown or "waste"

The structure of an IM system, taking into account IT governance and risk management, assumes that processes and / or tools that allow the organisational units / departments responsible for risk management projects to go through the steps outlined above, are available. ***The most important criteria are to identify the truly relevant data and application of the security measures on this figure.*** This is aimed at avoiding the protection of ROT (redundant, obsolete or trivial) data.

2.2 Information Management

Bruno Wildhaber / Jürg Hagmann / Stephan Holländer

2.2.1 Definitions

In Chapter 1, it was shown that the strategic use of information for most organisations occupies a strategic position, and if not done so already, will become one in the future. These activities can be summarised by the term "Information Management"

Information Management (IM) – The activities and organisational functions that are necessary in order to manage, control, and discard corporate data in any form – regardless of its media, source, origin, and quality. It ensures that information is accessible by all possible authorised users. Information management creates value and ensures that the statutory and regulatory requirements can be maintained at any time.
Information – Data which, through analysis, interpretation, or combination, creates value for the company.

Information relevant to IM is that which can be processed as artefacts. The definition has been deliberately limited to this scope. IM does not deal with knowledge that cannot be processed. Knowledge Management (KM) is a separate discipline and an enabler of IM but includes other branches of science which are not discussed here. It should be noted that knowledge is not a higher form of information ("information is knowledge in action"), but a concept that takes into account that explicit knowledge does not exist by itself (Polanyi[2]) it is purely implicit

[2] While tacit knowledge can be possessed by itself, explicit knowledge must rely on being tacitly understood and applied. Hence all knowledge is either tacit or rooted in tacit knowledge. A wholly explicit knowledge is unthinkable.» (Michael Polanyi, Knowing and being)

(experience, talent). The structure of IM presented here is as follows:

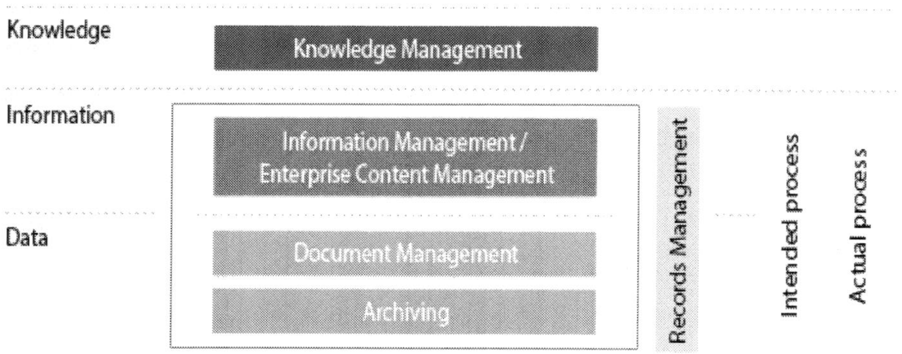

Fig. 8: From data to knowledge

It is evident that Records Management (RM) is a cross-sectional topic within IM (see the comprehensive discussion in the following chapter). RM is concerned with the protection of information / data over its entire lifecycle (creation until disposal) for the purpose of compliance (i.e. regulatory compliance) and includes all uses of data (see chapter 2.3). The industry term ECM is no longer used as the discipline is the same as that of IM, except that it is used in connection with products (IT solutions, applications). IM is a management discipline, the responsibility of each employee and must not be used in relation to buying a product. ("Every business is an information business".)

Information Governance will be discussed in more detail in Chapter 2.4

2.2.2 The Information Lifecycle Management Concept (ILM)

The introduction and optimization of a program for records and information management is an important element of a governance initiative and only possible if we take into account the entire lifecycle of documents and information. In general, there are three distinct phases of the information life cycle which are used to determine access frequency or value of use:

- Active (dynamic) phase: regular use of data and information to run the business (frequent changes in the data such as format, metadata, or physical form)
- Semi-active phase: occasional or rare use with low access frequency
- Inactive (static) phase: Those records no longer required for the conduct of daily business but there is a legal or regulatory duty to preserve them.

ILM means the efficient management of data and information from its creation through to use and disposal, archiving, or deletion. Various information-oriented trade associations have introduced the term "Information Lifecycle Management & Governance" (ILMG) in order to replace the outdated term "records management" (see below chapter 2.3 Records management).

In a narrower sense, the term ILM is also used in IT to refer to the concept of tiered storage. This concept is based on a passive analysis of data usage. When it is no longer needed data automatically migrates to a lower level of storage media (slower and cheaper). The business meaning of data is not relevant for storage solutions. They are therefore only recommended if the evaluation of data (taxonomy, business classification scheme) has been carried out.

From an IT perspective, there are very specific models or strategic introduction approaches that include project management and test concepts for quality assurance of ILM.

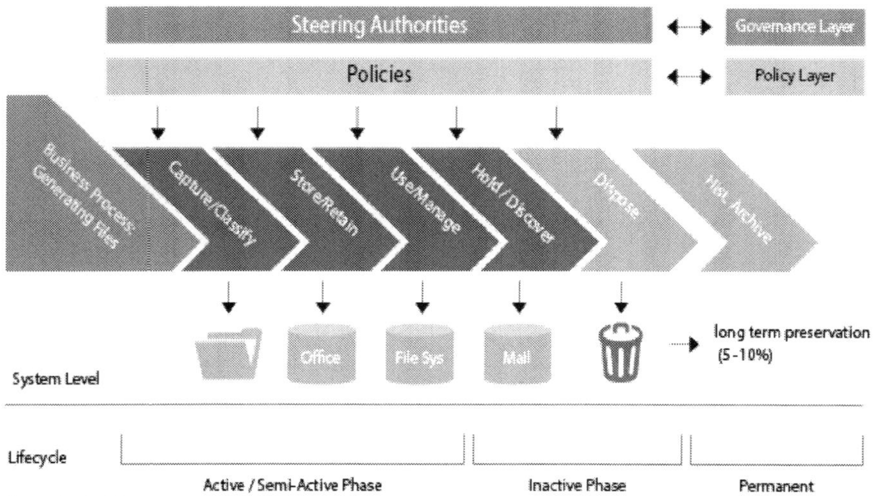

Fig. 9: ILM

2.2.3 The Information elephant

The information elephant is a graphical representation to raise the awareness of how companies ought to manage their information's lifecycle. It is a model that depicts the information flows and lessons derived from these flows.

The image of the elephant illustrates what features it takes for an organism (i.e. an organisation) to handle information correctly. "Correctly", here, means a manner that will meet and satisfy the organism's needs (i.e. corporate strategy) optimum:

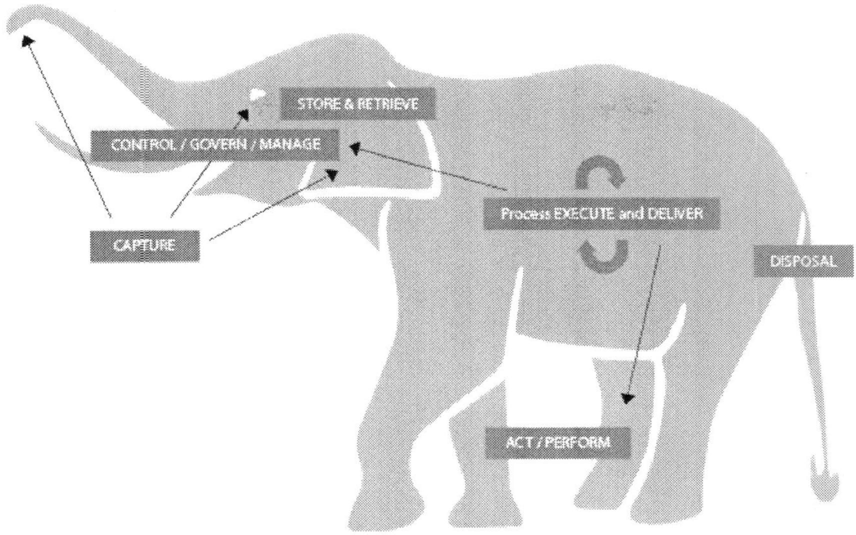

Fig. 10: Information elephant

Each company / organisation is similar to this elephant. Companies behave like living like organisms. Their essential processes include the recording, saving, processing, retrieving (or retrieval), and disposing (or disposal) of information / data.

What seems obvious at this point is not necessarily understood by the organisation or company. While the elephant knows exactly what he's doing when he is eating (eating food it deems of adequate quality), the same cannot always be said of companies. The supply of data is usually uncontrolled and flows in through more than one channel. A controlled and channelled input of data would be desirable but would be difficult to implement in the real world. As seen in the introduction, the number of data sources is constantly growing. The situation is similar with the evaluation of received data. The elephant must consider whether the food it eats can be digested. Again, this is only partly true for an organisation. Much of the data collected thoughtlessly is neither useful nor helpful to a necessary function. Under certain circumstances, the data may be dangerous or cause harm to the company. While the elephant has a clear ability to distinguish good food from bad food, for organisations this is rarely the case. If one does not develop this specific skill, then almost all data can freely flow into the organisation. The recorded food / data will then be stored within the elephant / company. The recorded data / food will then be turned into internal substances. If harmful substances enter the body, they must be discarded as quickly as possible. Data not labelled as harmful may forever reside inside the company. It is therefore necessary to distinguish the "life expectancy" and nature of the data that is collected and stored.

The processing of data in accordance with previously defined procedures depends on the needs of customers. This process is not optimal in most companies. Data is converted into information that should be available to the organisation at any time. It should be possible to access all the information and thus generate new information (business intelligence) to make relevant business decisions.

After the processing and use of resources the data is generally held for a long time in special memory (i.e. archives) or disposed of. From experience it is evident that the latter rarely occurs systematically within a company. Data that enters the body uncontrolled will usually not be removed.

Lesson learned: organisations which are able to get rid of data in a controlled way are also able to master the information lifecycle.

Organisations have a decisive advantage over competitors when they are able to:

- Tailor their information supply in accordance to their needs.
- Separate useful/required data from ROT (redundant, outdated, trivial).
- Ensure permanent access to relevant data
- Generate information from internal and external resources.
- Defend against unjustified claims.
- Meet legal documentation requirements and can present evidence in the proper form.
- Eliminate expired data promptly instead of keeping it forever.

Often it is found that individual functions and activities exist while the overall system or sum of individual functions is hardly recognizable. This has to do with the segregation of duties and the division of labour in organisations; one of the biggest obstacles encountered in practice. Just as the elephant cannot survive if its cells do not communicate with each other, so a strategic decision cannot lead to a positive result if the difference resources and forces in the company are not coordinated and bound together. The situation is even more dramatic: if the individual organs function but do not master the control system and data, the organism sooner or later perishes as a direct result of the uncoordinated activities of the organs.

The functions described in the generic model can be transferred to the lifecycle concept and show in the following manner:

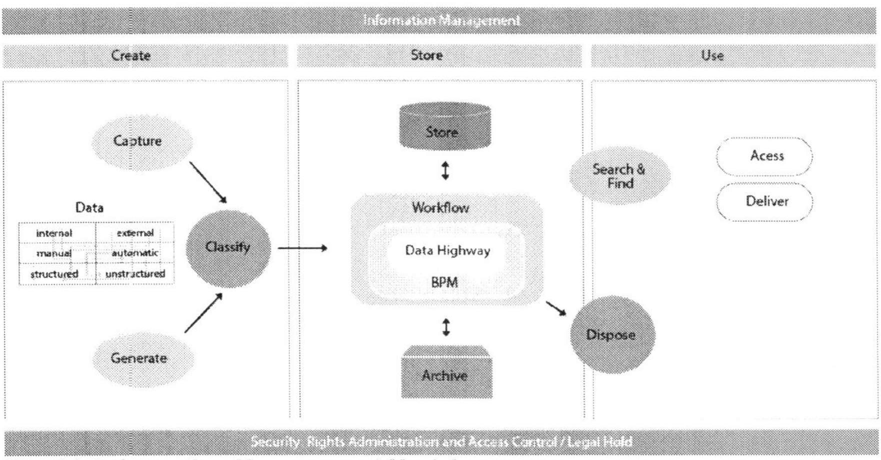

Fig. 11: Information Management Model

This image represents the primary goal of IM, namely, to ensure the widest possible permanent and timely access to all necessary information, regardless of its form and where it is are stored. An overarching consideration is that isolated data silos have no right to exist (except for databases which need to be separated for security reasons).

Data input is either structured or unstructured data and comes from internal applications, third-party sources, or created by employees. In principle, data can arise in the following combinations:

Internal	External
Manual	Automatic
Structured	Unstructured

For example: Data is created internally using a spreadsheet program in an unstructured manner, not necessarily following the existing business logic. In contrast to this, external data can be automatically captured and structured for automated processing according to clear guidelines.

It is essential to note the media is neutral, i.e. the form of data storage is irrelevant (with the exception of archive media which is explicitly defined in retention regulations). This becomes an issue when data must be disposed of. In order to achieve compliance with statutory requirements, all forms of data must be deleted – not just the physical. Customer files must be physically destroyed and the electronic data must be deleted along with data in backup files. The classification of the information by content is mandatory and should be maintained as a part of document lifecycle management. Classification can be done manually or automatically, and forms a key function of all IM systems. Classification means assigning predefined keywords to the information selected to facilitate the storing and searching for information. Classification is performed using "taxonomies" (see 4.3.4), i.e. catalogues of company-specific keywords, which are usually based on the business logic (structure of business processes) of the company.

Example: Early capturing of documents is the key to success, i.e. only through the immediate identification of data may it be promptly disposed of at the end of the life cycle or correctly archived.

This is true especially in the case of projects. Frequently project staff is the only people who have a rich contextual knowledge of the processed data. This knowledge is not generally available and must be drawn up later in a tedious and expensive manner.

At the end of the project, this data should be recorded and documented transparently.

The storing of data commences at the time of creation and depending on its life cycle and the legal and operational requirements is stored on special media or using defined processes.

Example: Capturing data upon-creation is a key requirement. At this point in time, metadata can be attached to data directly and accurately. This assumes that a corporate taxonomy exists to allow the capture of business-related metadata. A variety of the problems will be avoided if this principle is complied with consistently.

In IM, “archiving” means that information is saved in the long term, taking into account the regulatory requirements and special needs of the company. Archiving duration, form, and other requirements are governed by statutory provisions or established from examining the company’s needs. For example, the minutes of management and board of directors’ meetings are archived as a rule. To access this data, specialists in the field of long-term preservation and storage (e.g. historians and archivists) should be consulted.

Keeping operating costs low through disposal becomes the central function, whilst addressing the concerns for data protection. Finding data that has been excluded from the search results because the search criteria did not cater for its identification is a problem. The delivery itself can then be carried out in various ways and forms, provided the approach does not contradict specific provisions.

Example: Data privacy laws allow the individual to request information about personal data stored by the operator. In such cases, it must be possible to publish only a subset of the data found or deliver specially processed data.

Additional management, security, and quality elements must be added to the life cycle. The term “management” also encompasses the activities and organisational structures of Information Governance.

Example: As always, it is essential to establish clear decision-making processes so the question of responsibility can be resolved. Particularly in compliance-focused projects, where there is a legal requirement. For example, a local subsidiary argues that a certain regulation makes it impossible to implement a global policy. In such cases, it is extremely useful to have clear decision-making and escalation procedures, making it possible to handle such conflicts quickly and reach a decision in order for the project to continue.

2.2.4 IM Strategy

The requirements of IM can be summarised and central characteristics identified in the following principles as applied to the strategic use and management of information:

1. Reuse of data:
   a. The creation of any form of data "containers" allows the recovery and support of various usage scenarios.
   b. A onetime creation of information enables multiple references and output recreations on different channels (print, mail, publication) for different jurisdictions (keyword: single source publishing).

2. Integrity of content:
   a. Versioning, security mechanisms and lifecycle management are some of the techniques that protect the integrity of information and data, and ensure a high quality of content.

3. Availability (usability, findability) of information:
   a. The appropriate use of metadata and search engines to find the required information.
   b. Search results are delivered and presented in easily customizable formats and without the need for additional effort.

4. Optimised business processes:
   a. Automated processing of documents is possible. Functionalities that must be supported include: Creation (lead), format verification, release and deletion of various documents and data.

5. Risks under control:
    a. IM is based on the compliance of data management with applicable laws concerning integrity protection, the security of data, its quality, and the traceability of the processing records management processes.

6. Universal access to all forms and content (including context in the form of metadata):
    a. Access to all information includes all media and forms of storage. Searches can be electronically supported (taxonomy and meta/search data).

7. Reduced storage costs:
    a. Real storage costs (full costs!) do not grow with the amount of data.
    b. Operating costs are reduced by efficient and effective searches.
    c. Active lifecycle management allows the regular disposal /deletion of data.

8. High quality of work:
    a. Better search results and faster access to improve work efficiency and quality.

9. Reduction of the use of E-mail as a method of content storage:
    a. The right tools are available for data storage and e-mail is used only as a communication system. Data redundancies are eliminated and control is improved.

10. Reduction of file storage:
    a. Specialised tools (e.g. Excel import tool) allow for the extermination of file shares and leads to better control over content, reducing redundancy, and providing wider access.

11. Support for the system of internal control:
    a. IM operations support the introduction of an ICS (internal control system).

b. A compliance data base to show the applicable rules.

12. Simple migration or shutdown of systems and data:
    a. Persistent data systems or stored data can migrate or be shut down with ease.

Migration is handled in daily operations using standardised tools as opposed to running expensive migration projects. When decommissioning is carried out, the main goal is to ensure that access and data integrity are in accordance with compliance requirements.

The development of an IM strategy follows the phases of strategic management.

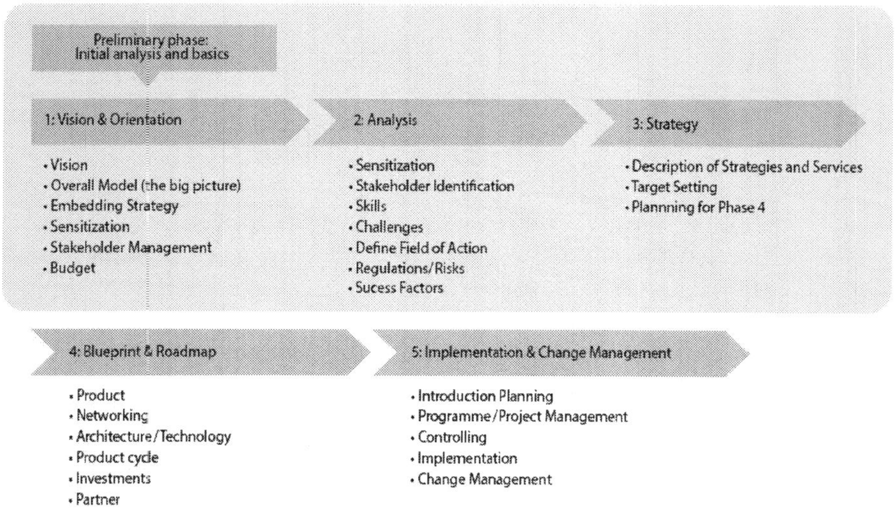

Fig. 12: IM strategy development

This model combines the process models of IM with that of the company's strategic development (based on the St. Gallen Management Model).

It is advisable to identify the IM maturity level of the company. The following is a simple maturity model based upon financial institutions:

Level	Typical Situation	Impact
0	The value of information is not known. The company works with traditional methods and uses IT tools reluctantly, on a by-product basis.	Companies without prospects for the future, who can no longer follow the information flows. Not attractive for potential employees and customers.
1	IT resources are used to support processes. They serve the everyday support needs of business processes or are the only way to handle such processes (e.g. Trading). No other use takes place. Data is stored in silos. The IM is limited to the classic archive / RM-topic.	Traditional banking environment. The weakness is the non-integration of databases (silos). Smaller financial institutions find survival difficult as operating costs are very high, process quality varies significantly
2	Information is concentrated in a few systems and cumulative (e.g. core banking systems). Data outside of these systems is not integrated or only by individual effort. Information management exists and focuses not only on compliance, but also on BI (business intelligence).	Many financial institutions are at this level. The classical banking institution that offers its customers its services electronically. Integration between different data silos is hardly possible. The financial institutions are prisoners of integrated core banking systems. Processes are mapped out well but require much effort. Expensive BI tools are required for data evaluation.
3	Information is provided through structured information management. Interfaces between the different applications / systems are open. The integration of business processes is ensured. Data flows can be established across different systems and security is ensured. Queries are carried out in the shortest time. New technologies such as Web 2.0, Social Media, etc. are used.	Lean processes and a comprehensive view of the customer allow the rapid design of new products and processes. Agile companies can respond quickly to market needs. The company has the highest ability to provide information and, therefore, has the relevant provisions in line.
4	In addition to Level 3, self-adaptive logic is added, which makes it possible to structure processes "on	Theory (Self-Governance)

Level	Typical Situation	Impact
	the fly" and implement new spontaneous visits.	

Table 1: Maturity model

Progress from the lower left to the upper right of the CONFPERF model (Chap. 2.1.3) is desired. This strategy is required to optimise the benefits of the IM strategy. During the formulation of an IM strategy, the development roadmap must be taken into account. It is always recommended that a company develop its own, specific maturity model.

2.3 Records Management

Daniel Burgwinkel / Jürg Hagmann / Bruno Wildhaber

Records management was, in the predecessors (Beglinger et al., 2008) to this guide, a synonym for the treatment of systemic or compliance-relevant files or data. The term "records management" is not well known in the continental European business community. This is mainly due to difficulties of a conceptual nature (e.g. Categorization / classification of documents in contrast to "records" (Files / Dossiers) and their implementation with tools (EDRMS)). In addition, records management is often perceived as a rigid and inflexible approach because the traditional records manager must understand and know how to structure paper documents and data in an effort to make it comprehensible for others.

In everyday language, the terms "document administration" and "document management" are used almost as synonyms. The term record-keeping has an official connotation that has never reached the private sector (in Europe). The term document management is used in Germany as an umbrella phrase for the functionalities for records management, archiving, document management and media management.

In recent years, the professional community gradually realized that it is no longer important to qualify and declare business-related information on any system or in filing cabinets as a "record". Some experts (including the largest trade association

ARMA) recommend (in the United States) replacing the older term “records management” with the open label “Information Lifecycle Management (ILM)” or “Information Lifecycle Governance (ILG or ILMG)”.

Here it is proposed that such a semantic formula be adapted to refer to the requirements as formulated in ISO standard 15489 (ISO 30300); however, the blurred terms “document”, “record”, “content”, “ECM”, and the like are only used in professional discussions and as such, generally agree on the overarching and widely accepted term “information management” as described in this chapter.

What remains of the concept and discipline of records management? Certainly all persistent requirements, namely the basic principles of records management (ISO 15489):

- Integrity: Evidence that documents have not been changed and are complete (time stamps, certificates, hash, signature)
- Authenticity: Is the “original” legally disputable (defendable / credible)?
- Availability (usability): during the entire life cycle: access, search, legibility, reproducibility, stability
- Reliability: credible, complete, and accurate records of transactions, activities, and facts
- Responsibility & accountability (ownership at all levels).

To those who are familiar with the classic methods of records management and would like to know more, the 2nd Edition Practitioners Guide “Records Management” is recommended (in German only).

2.4 Information Governance

Jürg Hagmann / Daniel Burgwinkel / Bruno Wildhaber

2.4.1 The Origins of Information Governance

Since 2008/2009 the term Information Governance and its expectations (IG) has rapidly gained popularity and has experienced incredible growth in recognition and relevance. The origins of "governance" in the context of information management originated much further back than one would think. The US expert in information economics, Paul Strassman (Strassman, 1995), has published amazingly far-sighted studies with the clear message that information-driven "governance" is intended to control all aspects in the field of information management including the active control of the generation/production, distribution, and use of information in a framework for the "constitutional" organised information policy (Governance of Information Management - the concept of an information constitution.) Although his approach followed top-down thinking as already mentioned, it is crucial that a clear distinction between IT governance (systems / infrastructure) and Information governance (business related content/context) has been made including all the consequences.

However, it would be years until such logical findings rose to the surface as the public discourse on information management is still dominated by technology (from IT) and individual voices like Nicholas Carr (IT does not matter!) are ignored. In 2004, the National Health Service (NHS) in UK introduced a practical concept (IG toolkit) in order to regulate the corresponding security and privacy requirements at various levels of their information services and controls. This example shows the complex application of the concept during its creation.
The genesis of IG is a strong adherence to the concept of Governance, Risk, and Compliance (GRC) which came into being at the end of the 1990's. This concept implicitly includes the management of business information based on a holistic approach represented by three dimensions: corporate governance (see Section 2.2.2), risk management (information risks), and legal compliance. Thus enterprise management, legal compliance, and the evaluation of risks go hand-in-hand. Accordingly, Kahn and Blair introduced the term "Information Management Compliance (IMC)" in their first edition of

"Information Nation" (2004). This publication – a kind of IM bible in the US – forged the term IMC as an umbrella term which encompasses all aspects of information lifecycle management under a coordinated and unified approach.

In this sense, "Information Governance" (IG) is "old (GRC-) wine in a new bottle" catering to the conditions and pressures of new trends such as big data, the cloud, consumerization of IT and other IT driven developments. The hope of a socio-technical control of all these processes and innovations (between risk management and value creation) is driving Information Governance. The biggest organisational challenge remains a cultural and political one: How effective is an organisation in orchestrating, in an efficient manner, all relevant processes and disciplines in information management as a balanced and comprehensive interaction (conversation) that is able to achieve the desired results?

2.4.1 Definition of Information Governance

INFORMATION GOVERNANCE DESCRIBES THE PROCESSES, ORGANISATION AND TECHNOLOGIES WHICH ARE REQUIRED TO USE, CAPTURE, CLASSIFY, STORE, AND DELETE INFORMATION (DATA) DURING ITS ENTIRE LIFE CYCLE IN ALIGNMENT WITH THE STRATEGIC REQUIREMENTS OF THE COMPANY AND ALL EXTERNAL AND INTERNAL RULES.

Information Governance is defined here to include the sub-domains of information management, IT governance and information risk management. INFORMATION GOVERNANCE is designed to optimise the intelligence of the company: depending on the requirements of corporate governance.

But what is a definition without a precise description of what is to be achieved? In order to enable a comprehensive and actionable Information Governance, focus should be on the following issues:

- What business importance/impact do data / information have and how can it be used?
- What opportunities and threats are generated by data accumulation/hoarding and information content ("Big Data")?
- Where does data reside and how does it get there?

- How can data be accessed?
- Who generates data and who owns it?
- Of what quality is the collected data?
- Who controls data?
- How does the lifecycle of data flow and what are the requirements at each stage?
- What is the best form of security to protect data that is exposed to risks?
- How can IG be implemented technically?
- Which compliance requirements are most important for the company?
- Where does the company stand regarding legal compliance when compared to competitors?

Good Information Governance must:

- Focus on the benefits “information” provides
- Always be subordinate to corporate governance (i.e. stakeholder requirements)
- Follow the four KISS principles
- Have management discipline at all stages
- Is bottom-up and top-down and, by doing so, must develop the subsidiarity principle that allows only those who are involved in central governance level problems that cannot be resolved to address independent units
- Be clearly definable
- Be technology-neutral and focus on data and information as resources (the other is the task of IT-governance)
- Focus on the defensive side of corporate governance
- Form an important component of risk management (as a whole, not only the classic themes)
- Address topics only if they are new and relevant (Big data, Business Intelligence),
- Allow for data and information to be the most important source and production factor,
- Should be on the level of strategic management and be taken into account as an influencing factor in strategic developments
- Focus on cross-divisional importance and the company as a whole
- Always be interdisciplinary and work-orientated
- Focus on physical and manageable / processable data (“tangible data”)

- Be easy to understand
- Avoid integrating and generating redundant structures.

However, Information Governance should not:

- depend on technology
- cover issues pertaining to IT governance
- focus on profit or strategic IM
- Report to IT
- focus on individual business areas / departments or business processes
- be overly audit driven and thus be perceived by management as "police".

2.4.2 Disciplines of Information Governance

From the issues and requirements mentioned before, it is possible to identify the following basic activity domains (disciplines) that must be addressed in the model:

- Corporate Governance as a parent guideline
- Information Management
- Risk management
- IT governance
- Security
- Compliance.

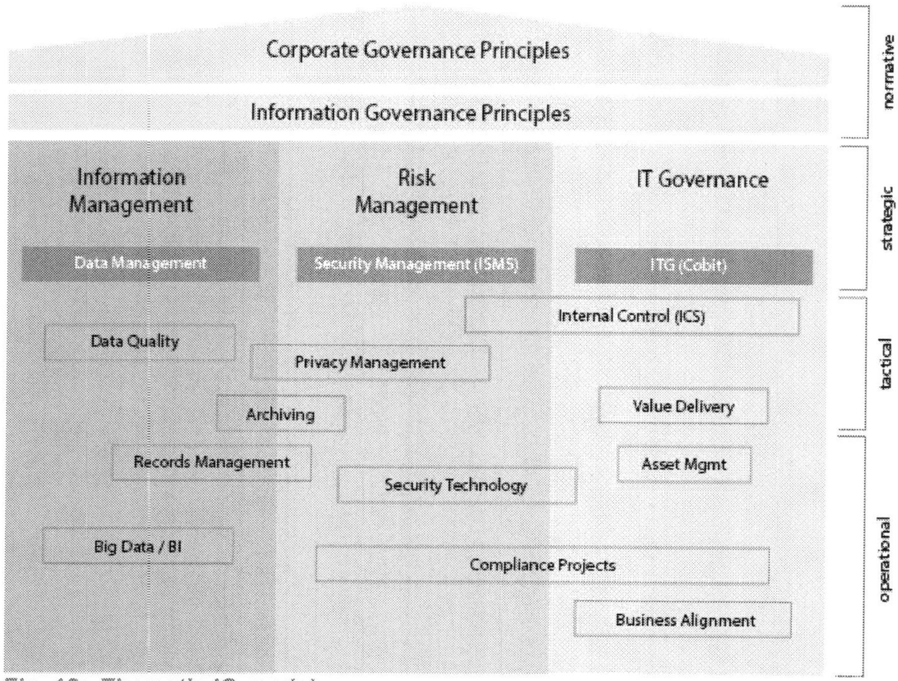

Fig. 13: Thematic IG model

"Thematic" means that themes are identifiable and can be described. However, it does not describe how the individual disciplines work together nor if the temporary component is taken into account. The thematic model is primarily a presentation of various subject areas. Each of these areas will be present in different organisations and their complexity will be maintained. It is assumed that these topics will exist in most organisations though they may exist in different forms. How much expertise must be available to each subject and how far the field is already implemented in the framework of dynamic considerations is relevant. There is the possibility that a particular department could be better equipped. If this is the case, new knowledge domains must be established.

Concept	Content	Explanation
Corporate Governance Principles	Basic guidelines for corporate governance.	How is the company managed? What are the strategic targets of the shareholders? What are the basic values and goals? Includes both the performance as well as conformance values.
Information Governance Principles	Fundamental values of Information Governance.	Description of necessary structures and objectives; Definition of requirements and means to achieve these goals at the normative level.
Information Management	Specialised domain that is concerned with the strategic management and processing of information.	Importance and methods of ILM, use of technology, IM architecture, project portfolio, standardization and control bodies.
Risk Management	Methods of risk management; specifications and method, core values.	Risk positioning, risk method, and approach in dealing with risks; use of technology, processes, and procedures, design of the internal control system; ensure data security and data protection.
IT-Governance	Rules such as how IT (information technology) is managed and controlled	Operational and organisational structure, goals and metrics;

Concept	Content	Explanation
		includes conformance as well as performance of the IT side, e.g. the optimum utilization and the use of resources as well as the value of IT

Described in the column to the right are levels in the company based on the application-level model of corporate governance (See Ch 2.1). This is described below in the dynamic model / procedure.

The specific topics identified have varying degrees of importance depending on the company and the intended use. In one instance, data protection might be given a high priority status (business model, which is based on the analysis of customer data) while, in another case, IT governance could be the most important element (outsourcing ratio). The illustration is not intended to be complete. There will be disciplines that need to be supplemented when appropriate.

2.5 The MATRIO® Method

Bruno Wildhaber

2.5.1 The crucial question: top-down or bottom-up?

Until today, Information Governance had an academic reputation and was considered to be of no real value. In today's management perception, non-productive activities such as information management or governance are always the lowest priority (if not explicitly required for regulatory reasons).

The current approach to records management has the following problems:

- It is regarded as elitist and academic
- Problems are not solved straight away
- No one wants to participate because there are no rewards
- No one wishes to be responsible

- It is considered a "never-ending project" – long term with no clear results
- Problem solving is rarely collaborative and therefore only "quick fixes" are made
- It supresses technical problems instead of resolving them
- Insufficient activity is not punished and therefore is the norm
- RM / IG / ECM projects appear to require a lot of work without tangible benefits
- The "data storage" landfill is not sophisticated but is a necessary evil as true costs are unknown
- The hidden costs of data-dumps are not reported, but are instead hidden within the operating costs.

All these arguments lead to the conclusion that it is almost impossible to solely employ the top-down approach to obtain the necessary funding. The top-down approach can be used only if:

- This initiative is supported by powerful sponsors (e.g. executive board, board).
- The existing structures, techniques, and procedures are already so well established that the top layers support underlying structures.
- The top-down approach is confined to individual elements, for example RM policy.
- Project results are not dependent on low costs.
- An extremely high, regulatory pressure exists which requires immediate action.

However, one must consider when the alternative procedure will be appropriate.

FOCUSING ON THE PRACTICAL SOLUTION OF A PROBLEM IS OBVIOUS. AT THE SAME TIME, THE PARENT ISSUES MUST BE ADDRESSED.

Users and management need to be introduced to the subject by developing the substantive topics starting from the concrete problem and proceeding upwards. "Upwards" here means that, from a particular point of view, further development will take place at the next level. This allows the problem to be viewed from the perspective of an individual, department, and company. Finally, it is possible that substantive topics be addressed at the level of the executive management committee.

In the example of invoice digitisation, one can easily describe how an isolated instance moves to the parent level. Electronic invoice processing is usually initiated by the finance department, mostly through accounts payable. The company automatically records incoming invoices and completes the bookkeeping process, makes the records available electronically and finally moves the invoices to an electronic archive. Similar examples exist for contracts and other data.

What typically happens when such a project is undertaken? The invoice workflow is analysed, the necessary scanning hardware is procured, and the formats in which these documents are to be stored checked. It is best to specify that these documents are not to be kept on hard drives but instead in an electronic archive. It should be clear the cost will include not only that of the accounts payable clerk, but also for additional staff from other departments. Consider for example, the process used for ordering parts, paying the supplier's invoice on time and providing a statement of the account.

The purchaser responsible must release the invoice and sign-off. The question arises as to whether electronic invoices are incorporated into the process and how the signature(s) can be verified. By now it should be clear that the majority of the discussion is important not only for this process, but for the various substantive issues that require superior consideration.

In this example, we can show that the following questions are not only relevant to this process, but need to be resolved in general:

- Which signature process should be used and how should they be managed?
- Who should provide the certificate providers?
- With which business partners is a company allowed to exchange and sign electronic documents?
- Is there a B2B platform that has a solution for this implemented?
- Can a solution be reached through a service provider or how many function points must be implemented to solve the problem?
- How is billing information captured and data transferred to another processor?

- How is the flow of information ensured and how can it be checked that the correct information is received, at the correct destination and at the correct time?
- What basic technical components are necessary in order to reflect these features?
- Are these components compliant with the IT strategy and architecture as well as decisions already taken?
- Who must access this data and how does this apply to metadata?
- Who is responsible for finding data and how is this done?
- Which archiving requirements are to be followed?
- Is there a problem with data protection and other legal issues?
- How is the new flow presented in the context of information security? Is the risk owner known? If not, who is responsible?
- How is the integrity of data and its information value checked?
- Can the implemented procedure be used as a default for other companies?

Most of the questions here have nothing to do with the individual process of "invoice scanning" or technical procedures. These are issues with the control and monitoring that must be addressed in the field of Information Governance.

What does this mean for the best procedure? What should be done?

1. Analyse the individual problem or the lifecycle of data / artefacts.
2. Outline a solution for this requirement.
3. Superordinate questions should be raised and addressed within the company.
4. Solutions should be adapted and unanswered questions resolved (if possible)
5. Escalate superordinate, not directly resolvable, issues.

2.5.2 The MATRIO® Methodology

Here the MATRIO® method is introduced. This method allows work to be performed through both the top-down and bottom-up approaches. Where one starts has no impact. What is important is the two-way (bottom up and top down) approach, which solves both concrete problems as well as creating the necessary long term structures (cf. the full description in 4.2.).

The MATRIO® method enables us to address the issues of Information Governance from above or below. It is even possible to pursue both paths simultaneously depending on the maturity level and needs of the organisation. Because the MATRIO® method starts from solving the smallest "problem" as a whole, it represents a self-contained solution that is capable of overriding principles and guidelines (Like a nested matryoshka (matrioshka 2014)). Each matryoshka contains its own rules and norms which allows for the application of appropriate level (within the meaning of the subsidiarity principle) of systems and solutions. The size of the matryoshka corresponds to the level of complexity covered by its topics. The top, normative stage is where the requirements of the board of the company are addressed. This may not be directly implemented, but can have an immediate impact on all employees (e.g.such as rules for social media issued by the board).

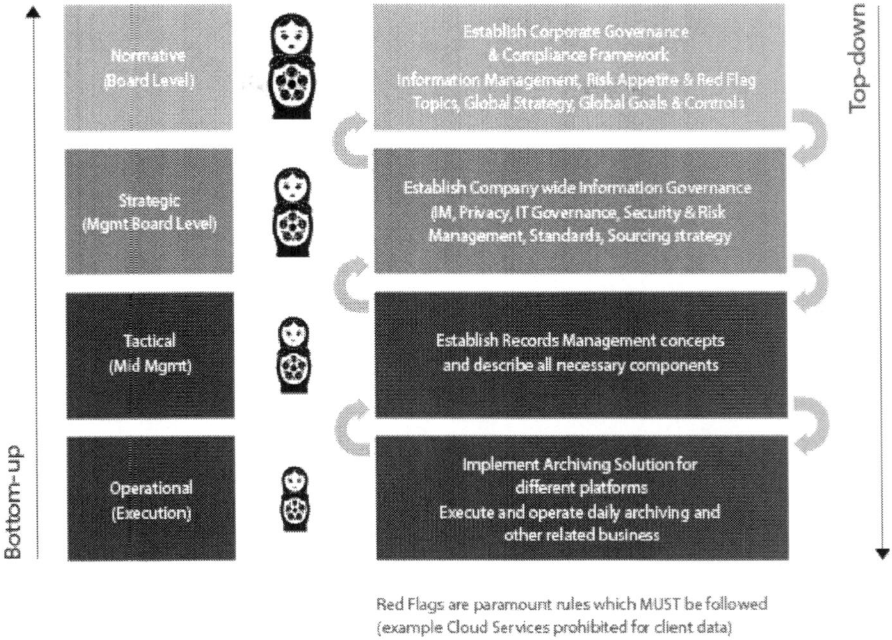

Fig. 14: MATRIO® methodology

This methodology has been developed in accordance with corporate governance requirements but also allows for simplicity in the identification and implementation of solutions in the area of Information Governance. Inspired by the “Elephant”, this model provides direct access to individual subjects of Information Governance and the necessary analogies.

This methodology is based on a few, well understood concepts:

- Layered approach to the assignment of topics and levels of decision making
- List of expert topics
- List of norms and standards
- Conformance requirement catalogues
- Performance request catalogues
- Red-flag catalogue
- Phase model for implementation (“cookbook”).

The phase model will be described below; an overview of the methodology and the red flag catalogue. The “cookbook” is located in chapter 4.

At level 1 (the smallest Matryoshka) there is an isolated problem or financial objective which is to be solved – i.e. a specific problem (called the "red flag": cf. the overview in section 2.4.4) - and the solution to the scenario (for example, selecting a tool for creating PDF documents). There are always at least two views, that of the provider and that of the customer who made the request. At level 1, more stakeholders come into play, including IT, who will implement the product. Emerging issues cannot always be linked to their overarching issues. Which files include this data? How should this data be found again, if required? When should it be deleted? Who else in the company should have access to this data?

Matryoshka(s)	Contains	Does not contain	Corporate Governance Level = addressing level
1	Technical solution; converter; memory; quantity framework; formats; process	Archiving legislation; dossiers; lifecycle; metadata; search criteria	Operative
2	Framework structure; legal requirements; corporate performance indicators; parent information review; implementation phases	Security aspects; privacy issues; knowledge management; IT governance; IM architecture; taxonomy	Tactical
3	Security aspects; privacy issues; knowledge management; IT governance; IM architecture; taxonomy	Policy; strategic importance of information; conformance value; performance value; corporate risk; IM strategy policy;	Strategy

Matryoshka(s)	Contains	Does not contain	Corporate Governance Level = addressing level
4	IM strategy; policy; strategic value of information; conformance value; performance value; corporate risk	--	Normative

The ideal ("consultant-friendly" = theoretical) approach is done top-down, i.e. senior management must fulfil their duties relating to corporate governance and make provisions for the use of information in the right context. There are various models that are described here (e.g. conformance – performance model). Corporate reality shows that, in many areas, requirements are missing. In this case the project manager or business unit manager can / must decide whether he/she wants to waive a requirement. The further one goes down, the more important single target elements become. Example: Without binding IG policy, it is not possible to introduce an archiving system. To address these cases, a conflict resolution procedure must be implemented (e.g. with defined escalation levels) in the project management process.

2.4.4 List of Red Flags

It is frequently the case that in practice, at the MATRIO overview level, the smallest issues in the operational sphere often create problems that must be resolved as soon as possible. Such situations or topics that signal the "red flag" must be escalated and, because they exist as "IG-topics", moved to a higher priority level with all the involved bodies resolving MATRIO in the long term ("bottom-up meets top-down").

The following list is not extensive, but it contains – based on practical experience – the topics which are most prone to problems and are therefore highly susceptible to escalation in an effort to maintain control of the situation:

1. Master data
2. Cloud
3. Multimedia
4. Data quality, general quality requirements
5. Single source publishing (reuse blueprint information, forms, and templates across organisational or geographic boundaries)
6. Standards
7. Metadata
8. Regulatory requirements
9. Backup (vs archiving)
10. Work flow management (e.g. digitization projects).

1. Master data

As long as the basic needs of master data for corresponding applications are being fulfilled and the complexity of master data is low, a red flag will rarely be raised. However, as soon as new applications or changes in existing applications / system / services are implemented, the requirements become complex.

If cross-functional requirements arise, master data management regarding an overarching coordination problem or governance issue must be resolved. Each value-adding function and business unit needs reliable access to the same well-maintained master data under the control by a responsible and authoritative party. In principle, an IG competence centre specialist in key data management is required; the solutions can be developed internally, virtually, or externally depending on the size of the organisation.

2. Cloud

The cloud provides excellent opportunities to test the suitability of an implementation for an IG programme and demonstrate how important are the co-ordinated control of various cloud needs within an organisation. All stakeholders involved need to develop a friendly and secure solution which can reduce the fear of losing control: the business (business units), the legal service with a data protection officer, IT with security and risk managers, data stewards, and cloud suppliers. How well orchestrated is the solution and is everyone pulling in the same direction?

3. Multimedia

Often business units struggle with similar format questions and problems. How best these issues should be controlled and resolved? A common thread in this area is the conversion of PDF to support a proper storage and archiving system.

4. Data quality

If accountants, IT-managers and agents are faced with large system slowdowns, log-jams, error-prone tasks and features, as well as problem areas, and "pain points" of transactions (customer complaints etc.), all relevant data should be analysed and the issues escalated in order to tackle the problems in a cohesive effort by all departments.

What are the problems and when do they occur? How should process rules, sign-off, and sign-in routines be handled? For example: change management, Lack of self-service / helpdesk, flexibility of user interfaces.

An important principle is to minimise the risks of "GIGO" (Garbage in, garbage out). This means critical information must be compiled promptly, accurately, and be readily accessible. Quality management should be automated as far as possible. Manual updates are always at the risk of human error.

5. Single Source Editing / Publishing (Forms management)

Single source publishing means multiple output formats from one source. It is a strategy of management to reduce or eliminate duplications and redundancies across an organisation (or at least a particular function or division) by sharing and coordinating reusable content.

Control of multifunctional usable source information (blueprints) by:

- Creating transparency (communication and interpretation)and identifying optimization potentials
- Define and design processes
- Implementation.

Additional topic: forms and templates management

By the cross-functional use of generic forms and templates, unnecessary office work (e.g. determination of properties, use of logos, etc.) can be avoided and productivity increased.

6. Standards

Are any of the following situations common?

- "There is an ISO standard that provides for the adequate description of these processes, and the company has reinvented the wheel with its own processes, what a waste of resources! If only colleagues in another department had been consulted".
- The recently introduced management standard does not match existing processes at all, what a mess! One-size-fits-all does not exist, but something like that must be coordinated!

To avoid such risks, applicable standards should first be made transparent. The following questions arise:

- Where are these standards? At what level of organisation are these specific processes (i.e. digitization degree of the company)?
- What processes are "standard"?
- How adequate are certain standards in relation to the operational requirements of an organisation (i.e. solution-oriented)?

External standards and the organisations internal standards derived from operational requirements that may be adopted by companies.

Chapter 4.2.4 provides an overview of a variety of standards in the field of records and information management.

7. Metadata

Metadata or data about data is a perennial favourite when it comes to information risks and plays a specific role, in particular, in regard to the following topics of information management in any application or system:

- ECM solutions / DMS (data dictionaries definition of a documentary reference unit)
- Functional integration of storage requests & privacy in the application (RM by design and privacy by design)
- Development of classifications (business function structures or IT security)
- Development of taxonomies (ontology)
- Legacy loads, retro indexing (bulk)
- Content Search, naming conventions
- Information education
- Workflow control
- File organisation / filing rules.

The better the quality of metadata in general, the better and more reliable the usability and marketability of business information (such as migrations): reap what is sowed!

8. Regulatory requirements

The organisation is always subject to certain risks if the relevant departments have not been informed as to what is required by legislation. Integrating an efficient monitoring system with a well-defined and transparent control and directing mechanism as part of the IG-program will help overcome this problem.

As an example in the pharmaceutical industry, a company was given a warning letter due to the advertising of a product via social media (e.g. Facebook widget) risk information was lost. In such cases, it is necessary that governance clarifies and introduces measures (establish a vigilance mechanism, instruction / training) to prevent such a situation.

As an example, a risk event from the pharmaceutical industry led to the company receiving a Warning Letter because in the advertising of a product in a social media environment (Facebook widget) the risk information was lost (this leaflet is mandatory). In such cases, it is stated: clarify governance needs and introduce measures (establish vigilance mechanism, instruction / training prevail).

9. Backup vs. Archiving

This red flag is often raised due to simple data loss from one or more storage disks that have crashed. The problem can often be corrected through a simple data restore.

However, there are also risks that are not so easy to fix.

Occasionally, information for a specific business context originates from a time past must be restored. In the event of a restoration by the IT department, the business must ask itself whether a particular context for the information (e.g. transaction, etc.) can be recovered from a simple backup while ensuring the traceability of business activity. Would a normal backup be enough?

In the case of a traditional backup, important metadata may go missing (i.e. copies contain only a date, incomprehensible file name, and hardly any of the necessary properties). This information is necessary to find and restore the data in the future. Normal backup data doesn't allow for proper information management.

Ask the following question to determine if this is a red flag:

Is there a simple backup strategy implemented across the enterprise? For which information is an "archive standard" needed, which would be legally contestable ("legally defensible") and has safeguards for its integrity, instead of a simple backup? Is there a need for coordination?

Criteria:

- Number of files, domains
- Versions

- Verification, authentication
- Period
- Cross-functional processes.

10. Workflow-Management

Section 2.4.1 contains an example of digitization of a simple workflow. The example of invoice digitization can demonstrate how to move the issue of an isolated substantive problem to a superior level of governance. The electronic invoice processing is usually triggered by the finance department through accounts payable. The companies will automatically (if possible) record incoming invoices and then make them available electronically for further processing by the accounting clerk. At the same time, a request is made that these accounting documents are stored in an electronic archive. Analogous examples can be made with any contract or other document types.

2.6 Methodology toolkit

Daniel Burgwinkel / Jürg Hagmann

2.6.1 Introduction

Every craftsman needs the right tools to perform his art; the same applies to the disciplines of IG and IM; employees rely on methodologies and tools that can be re-used in a flexible way to enable tasks.

The methodologies and models shown in this chapter can be combined and used as a toolkit. There are different types of tools and methodologies that will be described below:

2.6.2 Generic methodologies

The following table refers to specific methods from this book. The "step" column refers to the MATRIO® methodology (cf. section 4.X):

Tool	Application	Optimal for	Not suitable for	Level	Step
MATRIO® Methodology	Describes the overall concept and the overall picture. Unifies actions at different levels.	Introduction of IG; top-down and bottom-up as well as a complete specification; allows the orientation for a target model.	Solutions for individual challenges.	All	All
Information elephant	Visualization of IM lifecycle. Used for training and for illustration.	Training, understanding all IM processes.	Non IM-related issues.	Strategy, tactical.	All
GLAS-Method	Identification of the	Awareness creation for	Deeper levels,	Normat	1

Tool	Application	Optimal for	Not suitable for	Level	Step
	importance of information as a value-adding factor in a company.	board members and senior management.	too abstract.	ive, strategic.	
Corporate-Governance Model (Hilb)	Representation of governance issues at the level VR.	Board/senior management.	Lower levels of management.	Normative.	1
IT Governance Model (Bienert / Wildhaber)	Simple IT governance model based on the corporate governance approach.	IT management, board and senior management.	Suitable for almost all stages, however, focuses primarily on IT.	Strategic, operative.	2, 3
CONFPERF Model by Wildhaber	Visualization of project / investment decisions.	Board management, steering committees, Senior Management.	Lower Management.	Normative, strategic.	1, 2
CRM Self-Assessment	Sensitization Mgmt and Compliance develop risk profile.			Strategic, tactical.	2

2.6.3 Specific Methodologies and Standards

The pool of specific available methodologies and standards has grown so much that it is hard to effectively choose the most applicable. The following methodologies and standards have been somewhat structured and evaluated in order to make selection easier.

Overview of typical methodologies and standards groups:

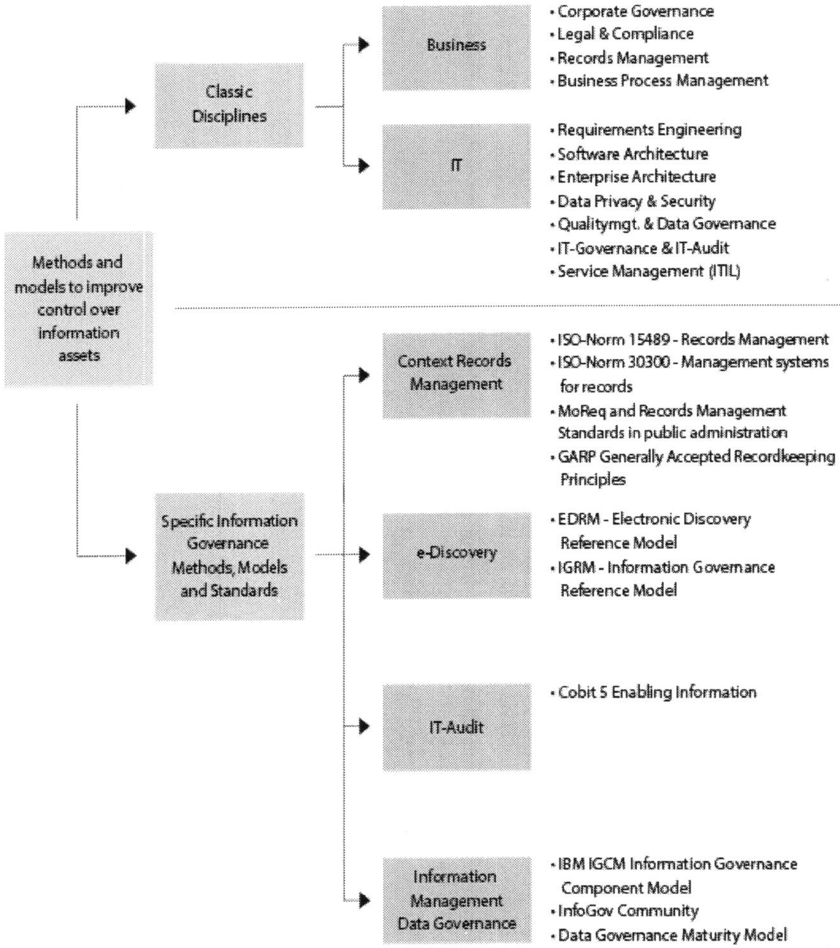

Fig. 15: Methods overview

2.6.4 Focus Information Governance (holistic)

Tool	Application	Optimal for	Not Suitable for	Level	Step
Gartner Toolkit	Starting enterprise IG initiative and roadmap development (IG program).	Planning a comprehensive IG Initiative.	Individual aspects and operational implementation.	Normative, strategic, in part tactical.	1, 2
Infogov Maturity Model IBM	Starting enterprise and function-wide initiative; IG; the business sale with practical example.	Determine readiness of individual IG activities; value; propositions of IG for specific industries and functions (CFO, CMO, etc.).	Individual aspects and operational implementation.	Strategic. Tactical, operative.	1, 2, 3 5, 6
IGRM / EDRM **CGOC**	IG; develop strategy / program; practical implementation of IG projects.	E-Discovery and legal; integration of all stakeholders; exchange with peers (practical experience).	IT Governance.	Strategic. Tactical, operative.	1, 2, 3, 5 7, 8
IGI	Studies and analyses of IG	Ongoing monitorin	Concrete		4

Tool	Application	Optimal for	Not Suitable for	Level	Step
	programs and events.	g of critical aspects.	implementation.		
Strassmann	Theoretical basis for the policy of information management.	Creating makeup, moderate Policies, and Charters.		Strategic.	3

Gartner's Toolkit (2009):

The IG model developed by Gartner adopts core elements from the existing strategic framework for "Enterprise Information Management" (EIM). Essentially, it is aimed at improving the coordination between the various disciplines of information management. All stakeholders involved need to collaborate in order to organise existing silos. The goal is to minimise costs and risks while increasing the value of the company by an optimised organisation of all information assets and resources.

The IG project toolkit (for IT leaders) provides the following components:

- Rationale, scope and definitions for an IG project / program
- Context and building blocks of solutions to all issues that must be addressed.

Information management must directly collaborate with corporate governance to:

- Use tools for surveys and assessments that analyse the current situation by launching them from a programme
- Discern which critical areas of action need to be addressed in order to tackle the business case. Decide which priorities must be set and determine who makes decisions.
- Obtain a template for the IG project plan, including a sample presentation for management.

Tactically, Gartner recommends taking small steps when initiating an IG program and first addressing the less complex aspects with the focus on the most vital records, followed by continuous improvement. Gartner warns of culture shock and underestimating the amount of effort required when dealing with interdisciplinary issues, political will, and cross-professional skills.

IBM model:

IBM originally developed a data governance model that is now being promoted in various publications by several experts.

For instance, Sunil Soares published his trilogy between 2010 and 2012: *"Data Governance", "Selling Information Governance to the Business" and "Big Data Governance"* based on the maturity model of 2007.

In 2014 C. Ballard published his "Information Governance Component Model (IGCM)", an approach for Information Governance introducing IG based on the elements of the original model.

IGRM:

The "IGRM – Information Governance Reference Model" was published by the association "e-Discovery Reference Model" (EDRM) in 2011 and combines the ARMA GARP principles with the process model of e-discovery, i.e. the management of electronic evidence in the context of litigations. The e-discovery process model describes the steps necessary for a company to raise digital information in trial as evidence, if needed. The CGOC approach (Compliance, Governance, and Oversight Council, CGOC; www.cgoc.com) is based on the new model of IGRM.

Pros: The e-discovery model assumes the standard processes have been established throughout the world.

Cons: The use of the e-discovery process model is only necessary if a company is involved in investigations and litigations.

2.6.5 Focus of Records & Information Management

Tool	Application	Optimal for	Not Suitable for
GARP Assessment	Maturity model for comprehensive information management.	Business, IT ›nt, point C ›enefits of e Mgmt.	Operational implementation .
IM Strategy-Method (Wildhaber)	Linking the corporate strategy development following the IM approach.	Business, IM, drivers in the organisation, currently mainly for visionaries.	Rather abstract, especially interesting as a theoretical model, for practical projects mainly related to the conformance / performance model.
MIKE 2.0	Comprehensive development of IM / KM-oriented organisation.	Open Source Projects, integrating all disciplines, architecture for federated environments .	Focuses on individual aspects; almost holistically (jack of all trades).
MoReq2	Records Management, ILM.	Determining the functional requirements, framework for testing functionality.	Suitable for the public sector

Individual methods:

GARP: Generally Accepted Record-keeping Principles (The Principles®)

The trade association “Association of Records Managers and Administrators” (ARMA) published principles for the proper storage of business documents in 2009. In 2010 this was expanded with a maturity model under the title “Generally Accepted Recordkeeping Principles (GARP)”. The association was created as a union of records managers, but the concept of "information professionals" has moved to the foreground in recent years. It is strongly influenced by "paper world" practices. Using the term "Information Governance", its aim is to comprehensively address information management and make the concept more attractive to senior management.

The GARP model summarises eight principles (The Principles®), which are regarded as the best practice in records and information management. These principles can be used as a basis for an assessment of the status of information management within the company. ARMA recommends this five-step maturity model. A technical report gives recommendations for the design of such assessments. The maturity model allows for individually designed assessments if companies do not wish to buy the official, handsomely priced assessment toolkit.

Pros: GARP summarises the main principles in eight understandable criteria.

Cons: Paid assessments. Books about GARP are available only in English from the ARMA association.

MIKE 2.0

Another approach to enterprise-wide information management is the MIKE 2.0 method which includes activities in the field of Information Governance.

Within the open source community Bearing Point (2005) and later Deloitte, developed a framework that culminated in the publication "Information development using Mike 2.0" in 2015. Supporting this is the 2009 Leadership-Gremium founded by the "Mike 2.0 Governance Association (MGA)" whose founding members include Sven Mueller from Bearing Point Switzerland. The objective is to develop an IM-centred organisation.

MoReq2

MoReq is the most important specification for Electronic Document and Records Management in Europe. The abbreviation stands for "Model requirements for the management of Electronic Records". This European standard specifies the requirements for Document and Records Management, as well as electronic archiving.

MoReq is similar to the American standard DOD 5015.02 (2007), a catalogue of functional requirements for a storage system in the sense of software-based processing based on the lifecycle concept and in accordance with ECM / ERM concepts (including test environment).

The transition from 2010/11 Mo Req2 to 2010 MoReq was technology driven; (for today's state of MoReq see http://MoReq2.eu/). However, there are hardly any further developments. The standard is not wide spread. The standard has been translated in 12 EU-languages, but there is no German translation. The DLM-forum (http://www.dlmforum.eu/) has discussed the implementation and value of MoReq related topics.

Pros: An organisation may search for functional requirements which match their own requirements in order to integrate them adequately into their own system. MoReq offers a framework for a test environment which is unique.

Cons: The concept and goal that systems are assigned a predefined "seal of approval" is not achievable.

The top management support for the introduction of RM often fails with change management. Predefined requirement catalogues do not contribute to this area. The trend in public administration is towards "holistic Information Governance" concepts (see new standards in Germany).

2.6.6 Focus IT governance

Tool	Application	Optimal for	Not Suitable For	Level	Step
COBIT 5	Capability model for information and related technology processes of an organisation.	IT auditors / IT-Infrastructure.	Content-oriented Information Management.	Strategy.	6

COBIT 5

“COBIT 5 Enabling Information” was published in 2013 by ISACA to complement the existing COBIT 5 Framework. It emphasises current issues in the field of Information Governance and contextualises them in the “COBIT IT governance framework”. It is described with an associated phase model for the life cycle of information. Further quality criteria for information processing, such as relevance and availability, are listed in detail. An emphasis is placed on the discussion of, currently, nine topics, one of which is concerned with three themes of big data. For each of the topics an example is described as well as relevant information, goals, and solutions. The topics cover known areas such as data protection, compliance, and master data management. The discussion of Information Governance on Big Data is current and is of interest to selected industries, such as the insurance industry.

Pros: IT auditing plays an important role in any company. The expansion of audits in Information Governance makes sense.

Cons: The introduction of InfoGov check points in IT auditing is useful but to build InfoGov requires processes in strategic and operational areas.

2.6.7 ISO standards

ISO-standard 15489 was published in 2001 as a standard for document management. Recommendations for the project approach include the introduction of a document management system (including Records Management). Typical cases include the design of file management systems and company-wide archiving systems.

Pros: ISO 15489 can be used as justification and legitimation for top management to identify important projects that set an international standard.

Pros: ISO standard 15489 contains a glossary, which is recognised and translated into many different languages.

Cons: ISO 15489 comes from the tradition of "document management" and is "theoretically" focused on records management. Aspects of mobile computing, cloud, and communication systems are not addressed here. However, the current business world uses these media for business-related communication.

In 2011, ISO 30300 was published which includes the introduction of a company-wide management system for records. The accompanying standard, ISO 30301, defines the requirements for an enterprise-wide records management system. ISO 30302 provides guidance for project implementation.

Pros: These standards set a goal for the introduction of a company-wide management system for business-related information (not just a "document management system") and provide relevant support.

Cons: Due to its recent publication, experience is limited.

Tool	Application	Optimal for	Not Suitable for	Level	Step
ISO 15489	Records Management.	Information-managers.	Implementation of an IT solution or an IT system.	Strategy.	6
ISO-30300-Serie	Management Systems for Records.	Records and Information Manager.	Lower Management.	Strategy, tactical.	5, 6
ISO 30301	Records Management (planned).	Requirements for the Management System.		Strategy, operative.	
ISO 30302	Records Management (planned).	RM project implementation.		Operative.	8
ISO 30303	Records Management (planned).	RM certification.		Tactical.	5
ISO 30304	Records Management (planned).	Assessment RM.		Tactical.	6

4. Implementation

4.1 Introduction

Bruno Wildhaber

In chapter 2, the objectives of IG are described in detail and methods (methodologies) that enable companies to gain control over their data are demonstrated. What is still missing is a concrete process to tackle IG systematically. This chapter includes both the description of the process model as well as case studies from different sectors and environments.

4.2 Application of the MATRIO® methodology

In chapter 2 the static MATRIO® methodology is described. In this chapter it is shown how the methodology can be used step-by-step. The process is always the same, but it comes down to choosing the correct level of management:

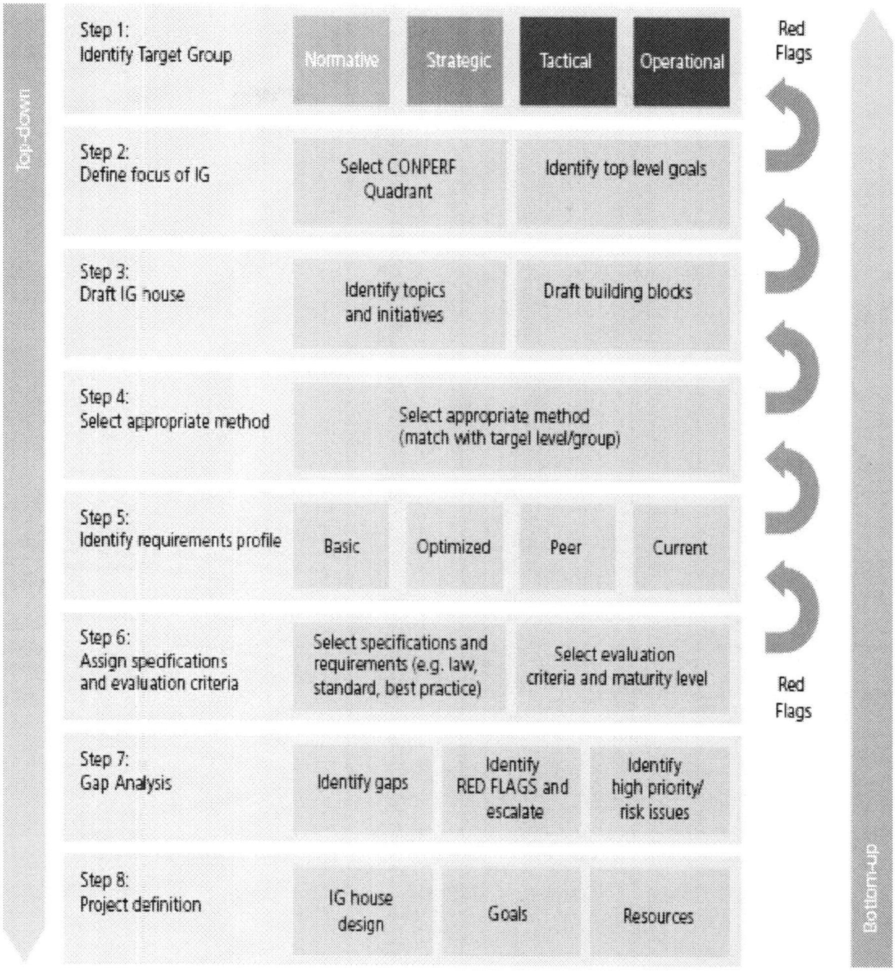

Fig. 16: MATRIO® step by step

The process from left to right is similar to the classic Top-down approach; the main difference being that at each step the red flag issues are evaluated. This will lead to the next step of the Top-down approach and a shift in priority. Special attention must be given to identifying the "quick-fix" issues that are typically defined in step 6. Often there is pressure, but short-term projects and urgent questions can be answered and measures taken immediately, for example:

- Can this product be sourced?

- Is this provider competent enough to fulfil the regulatory requirements?
- Does this technology or contract model ever come into question? (for example cloud computing with data storage in a non-EU area) Red flag issue No. 2.

The individual steps are described in the approach so that their core content is known. The complete method can be found at Wildhaber Consulting.

4.2.1 Step 1: Identify a Target Group

In step 1, the foundation is laid for further steps. The identification of the target group is important as it will have implications further down the process. Furthermore, the identification of the target groups serves as an important entry into discussions and to address the appropriate parties. It should also be clear from previous chapters that initial initiatives occur at all levels. However addressing the factors at the right level is the key to success for the entire course of action.

Toolbox: GLAS-Model/ Information Elephant/Awareness-Presentation/Peer Reviews/ Market Studies

---

4.2.2 Step 2: Focus Objectives

The focus of the IG initiative should be placed on the CONFPERF overview. This step, at first glance does not appear to be of great importance. But again and again it is found that it is essential to clearly define the motivation and objectives of any initiative. This guide refers to the CONFPERF graphic standard as well as examples from the information management strategy paper. The positioning of projects in the CONFPERF-quadrant at this time only allows for a qualitative statement. In order to produce a quantitative meaning from qualitative statements it is necessary to observe and collect the appropriate responses and measurements. It is not enough to solely imagine the numbers, these points need to be backed by quantitative (tangible) targets.

Toolbox: GLAS-Model/ CONFPERF-Diagram/ KGI and KPI/ Target Description/ Net mapping (Hoenegger, 2008)

4.2.3 Step 3 IG-Home Outline

The static subjects of IG are addressed using the IG-House (p..42 above) However the specific details are too advanced to be included in this section. For reference see comments from section 2.4. It is recommended that companies do not generalise issues or assume they are simple. At this step, it will be seen whether the correct target groups and issues were identified in steps 1 and 2. If a special issue has arisen, which has not been discussed in the context of the first steps then re-evaluation is necessary.

Tool Box: IG-House/ GARP/ IDRM/ IM-Strategy Guide

4.2.4 Step 4: Select Methodologies

This is the step which can vary greatly depending on the chosen initiative. The selection of a method refers to the method which will be used to achieve the core goals of Information Governance. As has described earlier in section 2.6, the toolbox offers a wide range of methodologies that address the challenges of Information Governance. Enterprises are encouraged to look closely and consider the context in which a project and its initiative are placed. The goal of the initial three steps of this strategy is to help determine the proper methodology (or a mix of it) to address Information Governance issues. It is not necessary to take a broad approach when the problem relates to a clearly detailed and formulated topic. The more precise the outline of the goals in step 1 through 3 and the clearer the expectations are formulated, the easier it is to select a specific, targeted method.

Toolbox: The technical methods and standards in the graph are discussed in detail in section 2.6 and are categorised according to the respective focus areas. Each method is a specific perspective that depends on the discipline and the interests for which it was created. While the GARP model of ARMA is focused logically on

Records Management and Lifecycle Management, the reference model of EDRM (IGRM) is better suited for eDiscovery.

Focus areas: Section 2.6.2.

- Information Governance (Holistic)
- Records and Information Management
- IT Governance
- Data Governance
- Information Security
- Other (Industry Specific).

Official Standards (ISO): Sect 2.6.3.
(Without Generic Methods)

4.2.5 Step 5: Identify Requirements

Once the target groups have been described and analysed, objectives identified, divisions set, and a method selected, management must decide on the desired maturity level of the results. Many of the presented methods have their own maturity models as such, it is wise to study and consider how they are best used.

Tool box: Maturity Models of the IG- Methods/ RM-Methods/ Norms and Standards/

4.2.6 Step 6: Specifications and Evaluation Criteria

This step addresses the impact of the objectives, scope and selected methods on the determined requirements. Here the maturity levels defined in step 5 and associated activities are discussed. Depending on the method used, requirements will vary in specificity. A pure management model, such as ISO 15489 describes the demands on a more abstract level. If the method is of a lower level and, for example, requires the implementation of an archive solution or the requirements to formulate such a solution, then a specific standard must be applied. An example of this is the MoReq catalogue.

Toolbox: Catalogues of the IG- Methods/ RM-Methods/ Norms and Standards/ Checklists/ Laws

An example how to proceed in Steps 5 and 6 including the corresponding targets is described on the online portal.

4.2.7 Step 7: GAP Analysis

The GAP analysis is an optional step. It is only carried out if the components of Information Governance already exist and their conformity with objectives is under review. This is likely to be applicable 80% of the time when encountered in the context of an Information Governance initiative. This means it is neither possible to assess existing components nor consider how they can be incorporated into current development.

Toolbox: Project Method/ Target Catalogues/ Requirements and Rough Concepts

4.2.9 About Change Management

Many Information Governance initiatives produce a culture shock as there are no corresponding business visions that support these initiatives. Existing cultures and competitive strategies for the segregation of duties within an organisation do not meet the user requirements that aspire to create a networked culture (Enterprise 2.0 - Sharing is Caring). Some fallacies such as "not invented here" or "Chinese Walls" may be revealed as counterproductive when they are shown to be ineffective in terms of a common and collaborative focus on the goals of an organisation. The biggest challenge is the inability of a single department or discipline to achieve the desired results. Success is only possible by a collaborated effort with clear value propositions for specific business functions. Such an effort requires excellent social skills, pro-active thinking and extreme co-operation at all levels. As a result of previous experience with the "top down" implementation of Information Governance programs, the relevance of cultural factors such as communication, interaction, collaboration, occupational interests, power, etc. are completely underestimated. If an adequate and reasonable effort of all stakeholders involved does not succeed within a specified period, then there is little hope that the Information Governance program will lead to success. The initiative must be evaluated using a thorough understanding of Information Governance. This understanding needs to clarify the following:

a. Perspectives and ideas of IM (IM orientation in changing identities),

b. Attitudes impacting information behaviour and permanent change management in difficult conditions,

c. Instruments (focus on controlling the implementation by meaningful conversation and interaction, architecture, language, habit),

d. Levels of action (finding a balance between desirable (people), feasible (technology) and viable (business)).

What cultural and business enablers can affect the implementation of an Information Governance program positively? The main factor is usually the everyday behaviour of employees and departments dealing with information and with each other, some of which are very difficult to influence (micro-culture), or the implicit, unwritten rules of conduct of the company (meta-culture). This is partly due to established behaviour and taboos that are known from knowledge management and which one fails to correct because the aspirations are too high. The following influencing factors will build confidence if they can be utilised proactively. If these factors are not utilised or they are utilised poorly, they can prevent or undermine Information Governance initiatives.

- Leadership with expertise and tact: Co-governance and partnership with respect. The role of management is primarily that of a designer, mentor, and modifier from the centre of the organisation and not from an infallible position at the top. The development of a balanced eco-system among stakeholders requires patience (instead of "personal egos"). This includes the ability to profit responsibly without authority (agile project management).
- Agile project management(*): Based on established trust through broad acceptance and goodwill, all stakeholders interact through "agile project management" which enables teams to develop better and more agreeable

solutions. Continuous work and team orientated consistency increases the likelihood of interdisciplinary goals being achieved within a reasonable time. The art is to use personalities to enable a climate of mutual solution orientation without misuse of power (hidden agendas) and manipulation.

- Transparency as empowerment and opportunity: transparency of all processes through consistent, comprehensible documentation is a requirement and all employees are involved in building confidence in planned and performed activities allowing for substantial morale and prospective cohesion.
- Solution-oriented collaboration and networking: enterprise 2.0 must function as a living organism; having well-connected, innovative, and constructive cooperation at all levels is a condition sine qua non, to successfully implement Information Governance. The "whole must be more than the sum of its parts". The connective behaviour of all those involved is thus the key to success. "The future of competition is not about out-performance but "out-behaving". How something is done is everything!"

4.2.10 Interfaces with other disciplines

The following checklist shows what necessary adjustments must be made in the individual functions within a company to implement Information Governance successfully. Although each of the IT disciplines listed highlights an aspect of the management of information, many companies find it difficult to obtain a holistic and current overview of all business-related information and to assess whether all important information is stored safely and according to Trim (regulations?){optimised}. This is where Information Governance must establish appropriate roles and processes within the company. The following figure shows the relevant business and IT tasks (IG environment).

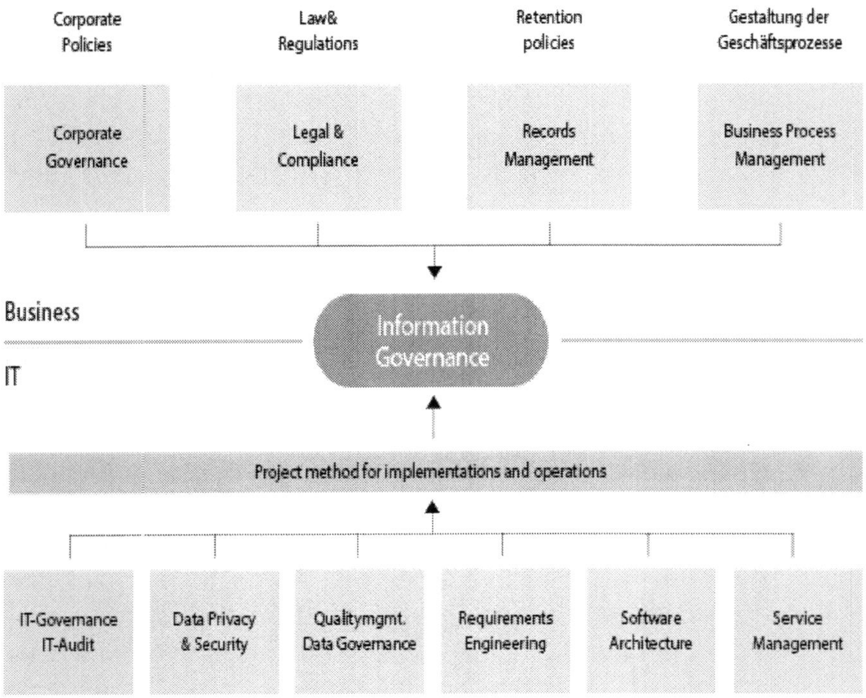

Fig. 17: IG environment

Interaction with Project Procedural model

The term procedural model describes the organisational and operational structure projects should adopt for the development and maintenance of application systems. Process models coordinate the activities of the different IT disciplines, such as the interaction between requirements analysis and software design. To ensure Information Governance compliance in the implementation of an IT system, the organisation must enforce appropriate checkpoints and milestones in their project process model. A typical milestone is deciding whether legal or privacy requirements have been considered in the arrangements for data and document storage and the duration of applicable retention periods.

Interaction with IT Governance

The term Information Governance is used to delineate the concept of IT governance and data governance, each with its own interface. In IT governance there is, inter alia, checks to determine whether the IT systems comply with the statutory requirements and support relevant business strategies. IT governance concepts also regulate the responsibilities between the business and IT organisations.

Interaction with Data Protection/Privacy and IT Security

The proper handling of customer data and business-critical company data is a key objective of data protection nd data privacybu and IT security measures. However, the measures can only be implemented properly if the company knows which information is business-critical and where it is kept.

Interaction with Quality Management and Data Governance

An objective of quality management is to ensure that all relevant guidelines and industry standards are met and checked in an IT system. For instance, in the pharmaceutical industry there is a close connection between quality management and Information Governance. There is also centralised data governance, quality, and accuracy of data.

Interaction with Requirements Engineering

The requirements need to be legally compliant and for the orderly storage of business-relevant information, must form part of every software project in the company. In public administration, the approach used requires the establishment of “Sample Request” catalogues for records management systems. For example, the DOMEA standard was developed in Germany and replaced in 2013 by the "organisational concept electronic administrative work - Public transport”. In Switzerland, a similar standard was established with the name "GEVER business management". For the private sector, there could be a requirements catalogue, such as "MoReq”, that provides a modular framework of requirements for records systems that do not meet standards. Demands on IT systems are governed by laws and regulations at the national level, e.g. in Switzerland by the accounting regulation (GeBüV) and in Germany, inter alia, by the "principles of proper accounting systems" (GoBS).

Interaction with software and enterprise architecture

When designing the software architecture of an application system, it should be determined whether all aspects are legally compliant and document storage is secure. With the proliferation of cloud applications, the question of country location is raised; which data is stored and what risks are associated with it? The discipline of enterprise architecture typically includes the analysis of business processes related to data architecture which require planned and documented knowledge on the information resources, such as retention periods, flowcharts and risks. Today these are usually not documented in the Enterprise Architecture Management Tool.

Interaction with IT service management and operations

The IT Infrastructure Library (ITIL) describes the processes for the operation and development of services. For additions and changes, not only do the IT technical aspects need to be examined, but also the impact on information objects, e.g. whether or not defined retention periods exist.

4.3 Records Management and Archiving

4.3.1 RM Implementation

It has been shown in chapter 2 that the basic principles of RM are still valid. However, a question emerges regarding the impact of the growth of "non-records" (e.g. chat or voicemail recorded as evidence) on the implementation of the RM. The central demands persist from management, and implementation consequently means:

- Efficient and systematic monitoring and implementation of the creation, receipt, storage, use, and discarding of documents and files, including the procedures for recording and storing evidence and information about business processes and transactions in the form of files (documents).
- Defining proper policies and standards as well as adjustments to organisational and operational structure with clear results.

- Availability and integrity of all relevant information during the entire life cycle.
- Properly archiving documents and files.
- The creation and harvesting of metadata, i.e. the recording and documentation of the origin context (context) of the documents (content) from creation to archiving and disposal at end of life.

4.3.2 RM-Project

There is little to add to the definition described in the method of Section XII.1 in the Records Management Practitioners Guide 2nd edition (german version only). It is still valid for introducing considerations for Information Governance. The only correction to make is that, in accordance with flow, there should not be IT governance objectives, but specific Information Governance requirements (take section 2.5 into account):

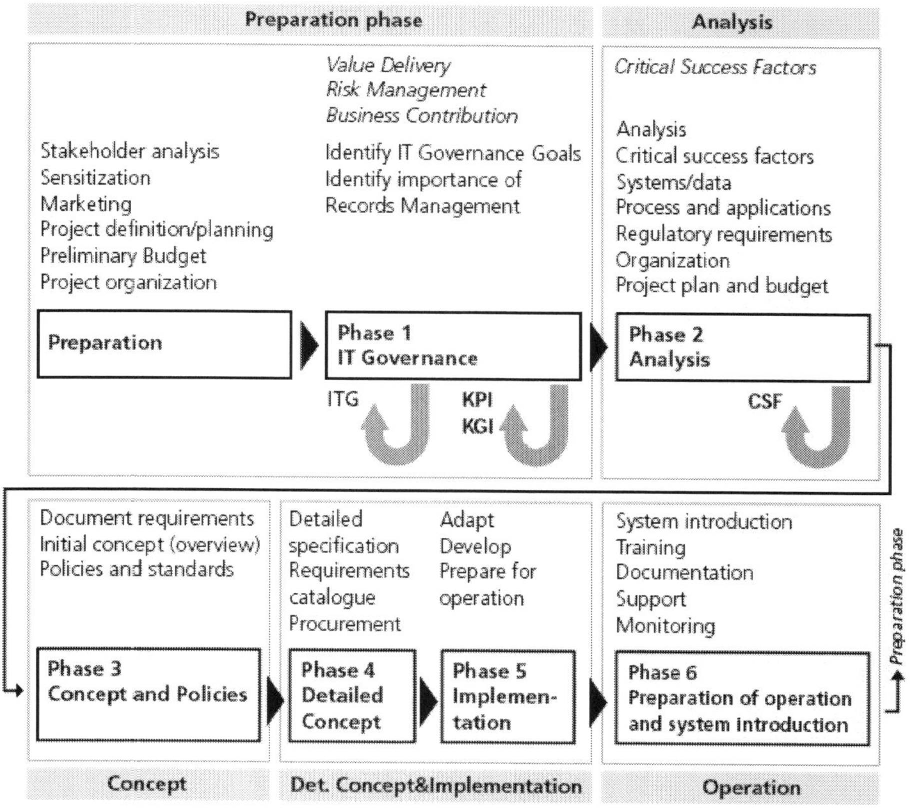

Fig. 18: RM project template

4.3.3 Important IG/RM Functions

Under the generic term “records management”, functions which support the proper storage of documents based on an ordered system are summarised. A records management module may extend existing document management and archiving system functions. Three major core features are important:

1 Management of retention periods

Retention periods and triggers are displayed in so-called "retention schedules", e.g. "retention 10 years after the end of the financial year". Retention schedules define which types of documents (above item level) must be kept under what legal or regulatory requirements. The RM system reflects these rules and should integrate them into its functionaliites.

2 Storing and retrieving documents on the basis of a Business Classification Scheme (BCS)

A BCS provides a structure based on business functions or processes (which originate records) for making retention and disposition decisions and for storing and retrieving documents. A BCS is the basis of a retention schedule and a file plan.

3 Merging of the individual documents into a dossier

Documents that are traceable are assigned to a business case. Other features include, for example:

• Controlled access to the DMS / archive

• Reporting on retention periods, document collections, and audit trails regarding access

• Management of digital and paper-based archives.

In the ideal world of sound records management, every business-relevant document would contain a marking that indicates the tracability of its transaction. For example, contract documents and customer correspondence would be clearly marked as “final” allowing for the identification and verification of the availability of all business-related documents to the business process based on the file plan. Currently this essential requirement is not implemented in practice, but is a vision of what can be achieved by means of records management projects.

Which IT systems must provide records management capabilities?

Since business-related documents and data are created and stored in different systems, different categories of IT systems are relevant for records management:

- ERP systems
- Document management and archiving systems
- Special or dedicated applications (e.g. contract mgmt or CRM systems)
- Storage of Office documents to network drives / file systems
- E-mail systems.

Many companies today are faced with the challenge of identifying relevant records from the large volume of documents and data in various IT systems and ensuring the storage of these records complies with legal, regulatory or internal obligations.

4.3.4 Business Classification Scheme / Taxonomy

In the Best Practice Guide 2nd edition, the term "taxonomy" is used to describe the structures used in the classification of data (Sect. IX.6). As private companies usually organise their data according to functional considerations, primarily focus here is the so-called "business classification schemes" (see above BCS) and the classification of the data according to business functions and processes. At their core, these issues revolve around the description of data or "metadata". The management of records throughout the course of the life cycle and the creation of additional descriptive information is called metadata. The term “metadata” or “metadata of a document” refers to information about the author, creation date, archive notes, privacy-related corrections, deadlines, etc. For particular applications and industries, there are metadata standards.

Metadata standards:

ISO standard 23081 - Metadata for records, defines no compelling metadata sets as these depend on organisation and jurisdiction, but there are, however, defined criteria for how metadata sets meet the requirements of ISO 15489,and at what point in the process metadata is captured and collected and how metadata will be handled in the storage process.

4.3.5 Future of classic Records Management

Due to the consumerisation of IT and mobility (Enterprise 2.0), the locus of power in the digital world has shifted steadily away from the organisation toward the user (Bailey). Consequently, a new "covenant" is needed between the user and the organisation; and the discipline of records management has to realign itself fundamentally. Today, operational performance is no longer possible if employees are too restricted in their information behaviour. Most attempts to organise unstructured information manually, at least since 2007, have failed. Attempts are now being made to tackle the problem from new perspectives. This has a direct impact on the attractiveness of an employer. Nowadays, the employee may reasonably expect to require discretion and flexibility in the handling of their business information. What does this mean? All useful and economically feasible technologies must be used so that employees do not spend their time on menial administrative tasks. The new challenges in electronic RIM are:

- Automated classification

- In-place records management & filing

- Folksonomies: social tagging

- Enterprise search

Such achievements will never prove 100% successful, but if the majority of data may be auto-classified / stored / archived / deleted, great success could be achieved.

<u>RM is a discipline under the umbrella of IG</u>

No doubt, the basic and developed methods, processes, and standards stemming from traditional Records & Information Management (RIM) are still valid and indispensable for many organisations. Almost all considerations for Records Management are included, even if they are themselves subject to changes in the modern understanding of the Information Governance approach as defined here. What is the significant difference? Information Governance is a scalable and efficient design discipline that allows the creation of organisation-related requirements and enables companies to find their own solutions. In the future, Records Management as a discipline, amongst others (e.g. information security, privacy), will be integrated under the umbrella of an Information Governance initiative (see. MATRIO® methodology, section 2.5). Effective Information Governance uses its combined disciplines to incorporate the conventional Records Manager as well as adding dimensions of flexibility and inclusiveness to the role. A modern understanding of records management comprises obsolete views regarding data. In particular, today all forms of data (and hence information), including (see. 4.2), must be incorporated in management considerations. This also means that many modern forms of communication and information processing of the formal categorisation of relevant documents threaten to withdraw evidence. For example, in chat or social media, it is questioned whether non-document format data can be declared as a record and how it would be saved. Thus, the term "record" needs to be made broader, but by doing so, it may encompass large amounts of data in extremes that cannot be collected and saved easily. Resolving ambiguity and effectively managing risks are skills that are found in the toolbox of a Records Manager. The challenge is no longer to present seamless storage - but instead it is to manage the gaps, and make use of a customised risk management strategy that eliminates unnecessary data. In other words: Whoever tries to save and control everything completely, will never succeed. It is necessary to create a business-focused management task that is based on the four basic principles of corporate governance (see sect. 2.1). Good practice calls for a reduction in data volumes. The sooner such projects are started, the better.

4.3.6 Important Elements of Future RIM Implementation

Each company must implement their RIM program and systems according to its own needs and standards. However, there are some key factors that always must be considered:

• Incorporating RIM into Information Governance is essential.

Information Governance RIM programs should be governed and implemented together with other related disciplines and stakeholders in accordance with the MATRIO® methodology. Overall key requirements and goals may be determined by the board, appropriate executive management or bottom-up, depending on the corporate culture. A sound RIM implementation mainly depends on IG driven risk management and well-designed metrics (KPIs) which are able to demonstrate practical success.

• Information lifecycle management is a must. It also means to value and treat "information" (content and context) as a real corporate asset which constitutes value the same as the other three classic production factors capital, labor and property.

Information lifecycle management (ILM) means "Bringing the elephant into your company"; ILM as a fundamental concept of RIM and carries the same weight as all other disciplines under the IG roof.

• Archiving data with unknown content carries unidentified risks. "He, who does not know what he archived, carries unknown risks"

The often-heard phrase that "archive to be safe" is rarely true in most cases. Keeping everything forever means, on the one hand, the destruction of shareholder value and on the other it reveals the enterprise's ignorance of relevant data (absence of appraisal capabilities).

• What is specifically kept must also be specifically destroyed.

To keep data manageable, it must be specifically destroyed when no longer needed based on policies. This is part of the records management concept.

• Marketing

From the first phases of a project there should be reflections on the "internal marketing" (motivation) necessary. The aim is to make the solution both internally and externally attractive. In records management this is a cross-linked subject that is often unpopular and requires great dedication. It therefore makes sense that the possible commercial potential of a project is considered at an early stage.

• Monitoring

In most (IT) systems, the greatest weakness is monitoring. Many systems are monitored insufficiently after starting operations and maintenance.

Those responsible need feedback on the efficiency and effectiveness of the installed processes in order to initiate measures (risk management, enforcement). Monitoring also provides the basis for the verification of IT governance metrics (KGI, KPI).

• Enforcement

Without measures to enforce concepts all technical provisions from a projects initiation are useless. This is especially true in the primary phase where provisions must be inspected periodically and enforced.

• "Technology alone cannot"

A company with the most advanced archiving system is not exempt from the steps outlined here. An archive system without risk management cannot decide if certain data is worthy of or ready for archiving or long term storage. This applies in particular to the use of E-Mail and other communications.

• Integration of existing systems and reduction of complexity.

Many systems contain DMS functions, thereby enabling the management of certain documents. System diversity should, wherever possible, be reduced. This applies to both hardware and software.

4.3.7 Procedural Documentation

Procedural documentation is primarily used as a means to ensure the auditability and demonstrate the legality of the procedure to a regulatory body. The legislator wants to make sure that the institutions are able, within a reasonable period, to understand the procedures, systems, and necessary components used. This requirement is based on the now commonly applied basic approach of "information system audits", as opposed to a "black box" audit around the system, in which only inputs and outputs are reviewed.

This of course raises the question of how in depth this documentation should be. An independent, but expert third party (e.g. an auditor) should be able to understand and interpret the documentation within a reasonable time period. This approach is similar to, if not the same as necessary for the applicable legal provisions (see. Art. 5 para. 1 ElDiV, old). Interpretation of the term "within a reasonable time period" may be disputed but the process could involve an auditor examining the documentation and then approaching the relevant persons with specific questions. The duration of this process depends on the size of the system audit. Normally it will take a few days, if one assumes a normal, average examination time of a regular audit.

Which regulations contain references to the documentation? Hierarchical provisions range from formal laws to professional recommendations, i.e. the "hard law" to "soft law". Most references tend to originate from "soft law", i.e. mainly from the audit practice.

In our view, this depends on the extent of the documentation according to the following principles / requirements:

Basis	Content	Example / Comment
Special legal or regulatory requirement	Is there a special law, which defines detailed requirements that must be strictly followed?	"Hard law": ElDiV and mentioned in Chapter 3 Special provisions for documentation (e.g. FDA for Pharma requirements)
International requirement, which was taken into Swiss law	Identical to special statutory requirements, the basis of an EU standard. Content often describes in great detail what needs to be documented.	For example, EU-Machinery Directive ("Directive 2006/42 / EC (Machinery Directive)," 2014), Annex VII.
Mandatory standard	Standard management, organisation, or an association, which is binding on the industry members, or members.	"Soft law"
Voluntary standard	Standards, do not assume the Best Practice approaches.	ISO 15489
Test criteria and standards	Test Guidelines Revision of organisations. E.g. the Swiss Fiduciary Chamber or ISACA. Usually expressed in the generally accepted accounting principles or data processing.	ISACA

The table above also defines the priorities of the selection of mandatory documenting content. Special legal or regulatory requirements must be identified and followed. In the absence of such "hard" requirements, the organisation may determine the level of detail and depth of the documentation itself.

In principle: The more critical and sensitive the function, the more precisely and accurately it should be documented. This principle can be found in statutory provisions (See Art. 4 para. 1 GeBüV or in ElDiV Art. 5.). In Chapter 3 the legal storage and documentation requirements of Switzerland were presented in detail.

At this point, the two main provisions, which are of central importance for all companies, have been nominally addressed and Art. 4 GeBüV must be referred to for more details on the contents of procedural documentation.

The legal requirement is:

Art. 4 Documentation

1. Depending on the type and scope of business, the organisation, responsibilities, processes and procedures, and the infrastructure (machines and programs), which apply to the maintenance and preservation of the books of the application, are to be documented with working instructions so that the accounting books and accounting documents can be understood.

2. Procedures and principles should be updated and the books kept for the appropriate length of time.

Art. 5 – Transparency

1. For each data processing system (e.g. accounting system) there is a method for creating documentation. The scope and structure of the process documentation must be designed so that a person knowledgeable in accounting can understand the operation of the data processing system for which it was created, without additional clarifications.
2. Master data and taxation tables must be documented. The lifespan of entries and any further amendments must be recorded and commented on. Further, enterprises should be certain that this information can be reproduced in a readable format without unreasonable delay.
3. The use of key figures and codes is only allowed for item descriptions and assumes that their significance can be determined by both the sender and the receiver of the data clearly, and without unreasonable delay.

New (As of 1.1.2010)

1. For each data processing system (e.g. accounting system) is there a method for the creation of documentation.
2. For the design and scope of the documentation to be valid, Article 4 paragraph 1 of the Rules of books Regulation of 24 April 20021 must be complied with.

Of greater significance than the legal provisions, are the principles which have been developed in practice and are considered a benchmark for the assessment of such systems (i.e. best practice). In 4.3.9 the combined catalogue of best practice principles is available for Switzerland. This catalogue is available online at CRM. The contents include procedural documentation that emerge from the statutory requirements and the specific company's parameters, such as business process, personnel, technology, and risk assessment. In particular, the latter has a direct impact on the nature and extent of procedural documentation.

Please note that due to the objective and purpose of procedural documentation, an independently documented procedure on all aspects (horizontal and vertical) components involved is neither required nor sensible!

The documented process need not demonstrate, for example, how software change management is performed within the company. Evidence of the regularity of these procedures must be presented as part of the ordinary audit. Here it is believed that statutory auditors are legally obliged to regularly perform IT audits. The standard documentation corresponds to an application / data focused perspective, including common issues such as management, operations, HR management, etc. The standard documentation describes in detail all systems and activities which are operated within the company. This includes the documentation of the entire IT landscape and necessary processes, including a description of the system operation, the necessary service levels, and system maintenance procedures or system development methods.

Standard documentation + procedural documentation = documentation set

Standard documentation and procedural documentation require:

• Process description for the basic processes and for specific processes (e.g. process of signing electronic invoices)

• Use of technical methods for depicting of this process

• Use of software for its implementation

• Lifecycle management of the objects and ensure the accuracy over the entire life cycle, with reference to the "proper documentation"

• Description of the control system (number of control points)

• Security aspects and risk documentation.

Part 2: Documentation of Archival functions

• The archive has 3 functions: organisation, planning, and operation (if not included in the general documentation).

• Measures to fulfil the specific requirements of the regulatory requirements described in section. 3

• Measures to manage and change management documentation

• Measures for the management of documentation

Here a distinction is made between the "Standard Documentation" which exists due to generally applicable documentation requirements and the "process documentation", which applies to a particular process, and is based on additional requirements (e.g. statutory provisions such as Art. 5 ElDiV).

4.3.8 Digital preservation

4.3.8.1 General

The question of the "correct" format for long-term storage appears time and time again. For legal, technical, and organisational reasons, the data format must be “readable” at all times without additional tools. This creates a wide range of possibilities that extend from the archiving of a printed copy to the use of proprietary storage formats and obscure data formats that can be read only with additional resources and occasionally require more than one operating system or standard interpretation software (e.g. PDF reader). Formats that are only relatively stable over time are not recommended (e.g. Microsoft). For large companies with proprietary applications, it is recommended that data be in native formats and documented in detail (e.g. XML) so that reproducibility can be ensured at any time. TIFF is a useful format too. For several years the possibility of using a PDF/A format has been viable. This format is recommended for organisations that need to store large amounts of documents. As part of a RM or IM architecture, the board must determine which long-term archive formats are to be used.

Warning: It should be noted that the migration of archived data can be required at any time. It is therefore not necessary to use long-term archive formats and systems, which have an "infinite" life. Archive migration should be planned and carried out regularly. This is especially true for data archived for 20 years or more.

4.3.8.2 The PDF/A format

Saving data in the original format on a disc and hoping that the data is still readable in ten or more years is not acceptable. Experience has shown that file formats play a key role in digital archives. Therefore, large organisations have come together from industry and public administrations to specially design a suitable format to be submitted as a standard of ISO. The ISO 19005 standard defines a file format based on PDF, known as PDF / A. This format provides a mechanism that represents electronic documents in such a way that the visual appearance over a long period is maintained, independent of tools and systems used for its preparation, storage, and reproduction. This standard specifies neither the method nor the purpose of archiving. It is defined as a standard for electronic documents that is intended to guarantee that the document can be represented reliably in the future. Consequently, the document may not refer directly or indirectly to an external source. An example would be an external image or a non-embedded signature of the document itself. PDF / A is designed as a series comprising a plurality of standards. The standard PDF format ensures no long-term reproducibility, nor the full independence of the software and the playback device. In order to guarantee both principles, the existing PDF standard had to be restricted and at the same time expanded. It was clear from the outset that PDF / A-1 needs to be built on an existing PDF version in order to achieve acceptance among the widest possible audience. As a basis for the PDF / A-1 standard, the responsible ISO committee (TC 171) chose the Adobe PDF Reference 1.4. Certain features of PDF 1.4, such as transparency and the reproduction of sound or video, are not allowed in the PDF / A-1 standard. Certain options of PDF 1.4 are mandatory in PDF / A-1: for example, all fonts used must be embedded in the document. The PDF / A-1 standard does not clarify the individual characteristics of PDF Reference 1.4 nor does it determine whether they are absolutely necessary, recommended, restricted, or forbidden. The PDF / A standard are continuously being developed. Part 2 and Part 3 of the standard have been published and address additional issues such as the implementation of the electronic invoice with the German [ZUGFeRD] standardization (cf. e-invoicing section 4.4.12). It is important for long-term archiving and for the ability of the IM that metadata is directly embedded into the document. The PDF / A standard is therefore an essential part of a comprehensive solution. The standard itself establishes no long-term archiving or re-productive parameters nor is it the optimal solution for every project. PDF / A defines the specific requirements for electronic documents, so that they can be archived in the long term. If an archive is to be established, which corresponds to the PDF / A standard, other aspects must be taken into consideration. This includes, among other things, the company's own standards and processes, quality management, trusted data sources, and dedicated requirements that are tailored to the specific purpose of application. In particular, the transfer of existing paper or TIFF archives to a PDF / A-compliant archive requires careful planning.

4.4 Technologies

4.4.1 Overview

This chapter is intended to show:

• How IT technologies and Information Governance can help control and improve the information lifecycle.

• The typical pitfalls, barriers, problem areas in the use of technology

For example, the use of RM functionality within SharePoint may be helpful and supportive. At the same time, there are typical shortcomings in the use of SharePoint as a document or records management strategy. With respect to Information governance, each technology has to control its own information and risk area.

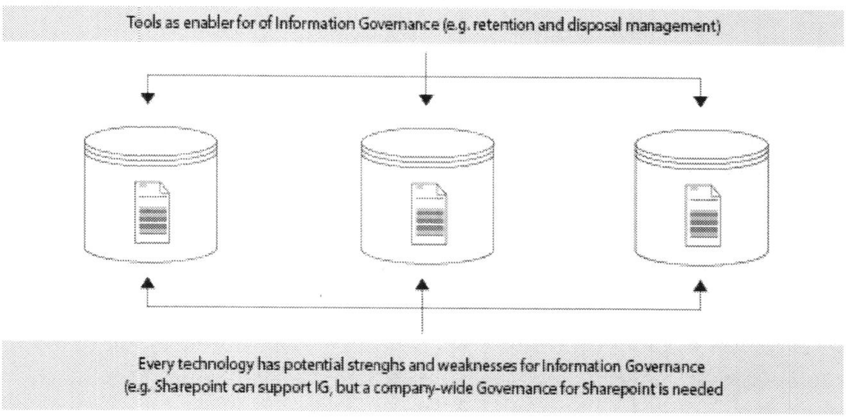

Fig. 19: Technology benefits and risk

In this book the following technologies will be discussed. As the technology landscape is shaped constantly by changing trends, only a segment is repeated in this selection.

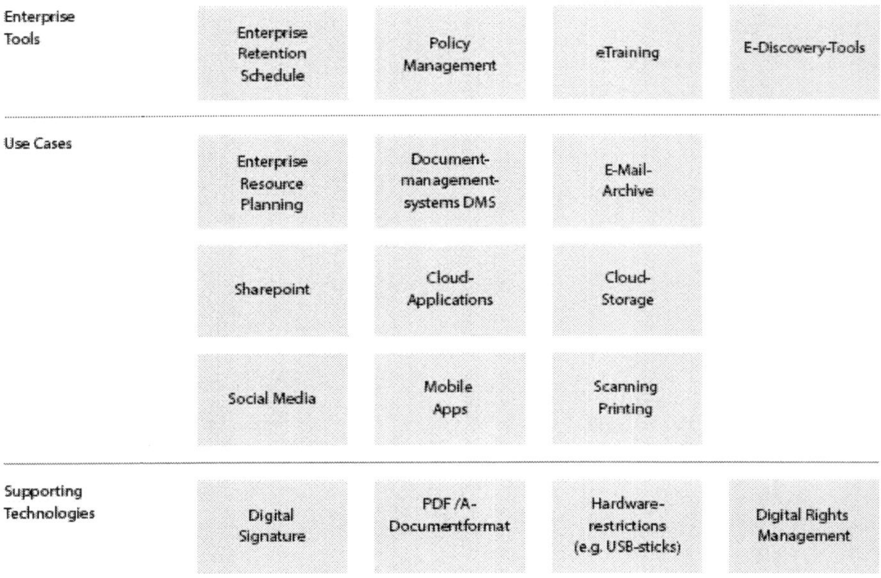

Fig. 20: Technology overview

4.4.2 The "Hot Potato" in Information Governance - Typical Construction and Problems

The challenges of Information governance will be illustrated below on the basis of the fictitious example company "InfoGov AG".

InfoGov AG did not clearly define how the responsibilities for control of enterprise-wide information were to be enforced until 2014. While the level of IT governance had been decided, questions appeared regarding security, deletion of data, and the correct retention periods.

The following problems are typical cases:

• SharePoint: Projects had been stored on SharePoint sites alongside business-relevant documents. On completion of the project the project leaders left the company. Soon thereafter is was discovered that it was no longer clear which documents were the important final versions and how long they had to be kept. Rather than keep only the important documents, all data was stored, which led to a steady and uncontrolled growth of unstructured data.

• ERP: Generally the company's management assumed that, in the context of the ERP system, everything was controlled and documented happily in the SAP . But the archive was lacking, in the ERP context, an overview of the processes used to archive the data and whether copies were still present in other locations. In addition, whilst messages were archived centrally they were not allocated with the ERP data.

• E-mail: In order to "play it safe", the IT manager implemented an email archive, storing all corporate internal and external communications for 10 years. Following this installation, it transpired that, in some areas of the company, business-related messages were assigned to the transaction. In addition, doubts arose as to whether all emails need to be archived, since the mail volume rose steadily (as some employees were receiving / sending up to 200 e-mails per day). An analysis showed that their mail was redundantly stored in spite of the mail archiving on the organisation's own servers for fast access.

• Cloud storage: In particular, employees who travelled extensively were saving business-relevant documents in the cloud (Dropbox, iCloud). When an employee left the department or company, the files remained in the cloud and were never deleted.

• Cloud applications: Sales had decided to use a cloud-based software solution for CRM. After two years, the question arose of the data should be archived. Because the vendors did not offer an appropriate interface, all content continued to be stored in the cloud, which led to a strong dependence on the cloud service provider.

4.4.3 ECM - Enterprise Content Management and Records Management

The term ECM refers to a variety of IT tools which are summarised below with a description of how each category of tool contributes to Information Governance if applied in an appropriate manner. There are two challenges in the implementation of ECM tools.

1. An enterprise-wide integration of ECM components should be implemented and include interoperability and alignment.

2. Every single application should be optimised according to interoperability requirements.

To successfully deploy ECM technology, an enterprise-wide Information Governance concept is required.

For the storage of documents a variety of systems in the field of enterprise content management (ECM) is relevant:

• Archiving systems for documents, ERP-data, and e-mails

• Document management systems and files / dossier management (electronic act: E-act, GEVER, and Records Management)

• Collaboration solutions such as Sharepoint that enable co-operation amongst employees

• Tools for the management of a company-wide retention schedule and file plan for digital and physical documents (a functional integration of lifecycle attributes is usually missing; see section 4.4.11 below) – this a long-running hot potato

• Data and documents which are kept in Cloud-Storage services, cloud apps, and social media applications

• Big Data: Analyses of big data collection for various purposes (e.g. the creation of profiles of users who visit the corporate web site)

• Electronic invoice processing (e-invoice)

• Digitization (scanning) of incoming physical mail

4.4.4 Document Management Systems (DMS)

A document management system (DMS) enables the user to manage digital documents. In contrast to simple storage, where the user makes use of a customised folder structure on a local PC, the DMS provides several advantages. In a DMS, the documents are stored in a structure using a general, overarching system of order (document title, version, date), making it easy to find the final version of the document. In addition, the simultaneous processing of a document by multiple users can be prevented by limiting access through locks for editing by other users (check-in / check-out). However, the main advantages of a DMS are in the processing and orchestrated forwarding of documents. These workflow capabilities, also called Business Process Management (BPM), allow for the optimization and acceleration of the processes for documents, while simultaneously minimizing errors.

Fields of application:

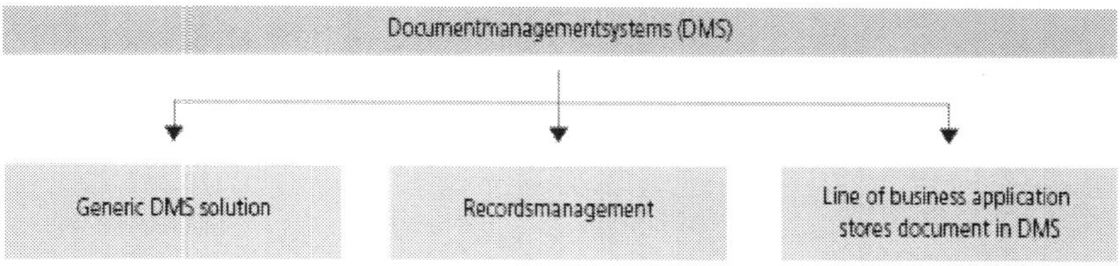

Fig. 21: DMS fields of application

Challenges in implementing Information Governance

Checklist	Information Governance of DMS
Business and IT (ownership & stewardship)	• If defined, who bears the responsibility (ownership) for the legally-compliant storage of the business? • Is this regulated when several regions or departments use the system (stewardship)? • Who is responsible on the part of IT for the operation and development of the system (technical ownership and stewardship?
Objectives, Scope and risk of the system	• Is there an enterprise-wide deployment strategy for DMS, e.g. a software standard or different DMS system per country / region that will be used? • Is the application area defined and clearly delineated? • Are business relevance, security needs, and data protection requirements clearly defined? • Is this a generic file and dossier management system or a specialist application based DMS?
Retention schedule	• Are the retention periods and triggers for

Checklist	Information Governance of DMS
	documents defined? • Are the legal requirements and industry standards that were used as a basis for defining the retention periods documented? • How often will the legal requirements be reviewed / changed? • If the DMS is storing documents from several international subsidiaries, are the national requirements met? (challenges of multi-national jurisdiction; what is the master schedule?)
Business correspondence	• Must both the business-related documents, as well as the associated e-mails, be stored as evidence in DMS? • Switzerland: has the impact of the GeBüV standard on a company's internal storage been examined (if accounting documents available, it would be the company's decision to keep the business correspondence)?
Document formats and Digital Signatures	Is the DMS able to store digital invoices in the future?

4.4.5 ERP Systems

4.4.5.1 Application Areas for ERP systems

The following three RP use cases must be distinguished:

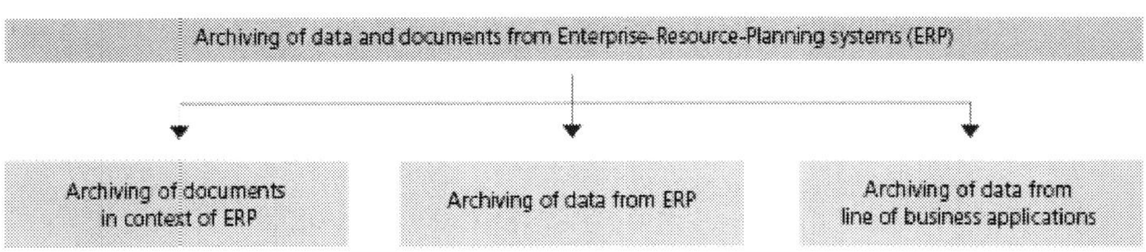

Fig. 22: ERP use cases

4.4.5.2 Archiving documents

In the context of ERP systems, numerous documents are processed, for example, supplier invoices, which are then stored in the retention / archiving system.

ERP	
Prospects	**Risks**
If ERP archiving is done properly, a large part of business-relevant documents is preserved.	• The importance of ERP archiving is misjudged; although business critical documents are kept, a failure of the archive can affect daily operations. • Expenses for correct archive planning are underestimated and neglected during the life cycle. • Employees create documents in other redundant directories because the ERP system is not user friendly.
Checklist	**Information Governance of ERP systems**
Country-specific requirements for ERP	• Are the legal requirements for the respective countries clarified? • Case Study: Swiss companies lead by accounting for Swiss society and German subsidiary. Location of the archive is in Switzerland. What specific German and Swiss requirements are taken into account? • In which countries must special functions be provided, e.g. in Germany the access of tax administration on ERP data?
Availability and Performance	• What are the compliance system availability and the risk of defaulting on business needs? What risks arise when documents in daily use are not available because of a failure?
Responsibility for Information vs. Responsibility for the IT System	• The ERP system can cover a wide variety of applications. Who is responsible for which information inventory, for example, compliance with retention periods?

4.4.5.3 Storage in Daily Operations vs. Archiving[3]

An archive system is designed to catalogue documents pertaining to legal or other business issues in an organised and technical manner so operational costs remain optimal and information remains easily accessible organisation. Archiving here is used in the broader sense as the fulfilment of commercial storage duties. As long as digital documents are stored in the system it must adhere to the functional requirements [specified in Article 8 GeBüV] regarding inventory, protection against unauthorised access and the recording of the number of hits and entries. Some jurisdictions recommend a separation of custodianship to be made (documents used in daily business and documents transferred into the archives. This can be done by separating or classifying (by using tags) the documents. This model is based on traditional storage schemes, where the archive in the basement was physically separated from office filing. For traditional document management that segregation is appropriate. By contrast, this dual concept is more difficult to understand and implement in a digital environment, where the documents are stored in an integrated IT system. A common method is the direct storage of digital documents in a document management system that meets the requirements of archiving standards. A document in such a system may be kept until the law [GeBüV] increases the requirements set on the retention of legal or other business documents (e.g. deemed necessary evidence). In this case the legal document must be stored in an unalterable DMS system (ensuring data integrity) and marked as current. Once the legal archiving period starts, a label must be archived with the document in order to meet the mandatory [GeBüV] legal requirements.

The term "archive" is sometimes used in practice is not synonymous with "unchangeable storage". To avoid misinterpretation, it is recommended that a company precisely differentiate the use of the terms "archive" and "unchangeable storage".

Art. 7 GeBüV, instead of a physical separation, requires only "logical" distinction between current and archived information

---

3 This section describes the situation based on Swiss Law, mainly the Trade law requirements (GeBüV).

through appropriate labelling, provided the other archiving requirements are met (see. the principles in 4.3.9). Because of this legal flexibility an archive system can be replaced by an appropriately altered DMS that stores current documents under explicit labels and then, once the use of the data dwindles, archives it in accordance with the applicable policy are relabelled. Companies must ensure that the mandatory GeBüV requirements for archiving are met throughout the archiving process.

4.4.6 E-Mail and Instant Messaging Archiving

E-mails and other electronic communication systems may be subject to storage. By now, this is well known. However, not all mail traffic needs to be stored. In most companies only perhaps 5 - 10% of the total volume of data found in communication systems must be stored. Nevertheless, the increase in the archiving of emails as a "journaling" system in recent years has reached exponential proportions. In journaling (actually that is a supervision measure) the non-selective, complete record of all mail data is understandable. To call this process an “epidemic” would be stretching the truth, but not completely out of line. From a legal perspective, the story is simple; E-mail is a means of communication and may contain data that must be kept whether it be in the form of classic business correspondence (which is no longer required in Switzerland from 1.1.2013), or evidence, e.g. in the execution of large projects. Such storage is perfectly acceptable if it is performed via the selection of the emails (manual separation) or done with organisational resources by intelligent mail archiving software. In any case, however, the number of companies that should be using comprehensive e-mail journaling is small. The conflict with data protection is obvious. Email journaling cannot be performed without taking legal risks. The best that can be done to protect the data is to use a common mail server for all mail accounts in several countries which are not very secure. The organisational measures around journaling usually destroy any benefit that could result from such action.

The authors are currently planning to set up a cost-benefit comparison for e-mail journaling which will be published on the CRM website (informationgovernance.ch).

In Section 4.5 the description of a detailed e-discovery process in which e-mail plays a central role may be found

4.4.7 SharePoint in the enterprise

4.4.7.1 Opportunities and Risks

Definition and Applications Microsoft SharePoint	**MS SharePoint has been developed as a collaboration tool and is used by many companies to support cooperation and as a substitute for traditional document management systems.** **In practice, one can distinguish between the following scenarios:** **• SharePoint as a collaboration tool (e.g. for projects)** **• SharePoint as a DMS for small departments** **• SharePoint as an enterprise platform (frontend)**

Sharepoint needs governance

Opportunities	Risks
• Availability: Corporate users may use SharePoint after agreeing to a Microsoft License Agreement. For the filing of documents, SharePoint is an obvious solution. Although SP may encourage the purchase of external software, it is not necessary. **• "Better than File Storage". SharePoint provides basic functions such as versioning, rights assignment, and selected RM functions.** **• Fast set-up. If temporary document repositories are required set up cost and time are low.**	Risks in the absence of governance include • Uncontrolled growth (sprawling) of the number of SP Sites and data volumes, since end users can create unregulated sites. • Lack of governance: Who gives specifications; who ensures that data is stored? What is the lifecycle of a SP site and who is responsible for life cycle management? • Workarounds: Instead of a implementing a proper solution SP Sites extend to include application functions and are pushed to their

Opportunities	Risks
• Addition of new features and trends: Microsoft sees SharePoint as an important product and further expands its capabilities every three years. In versions SP 2010, SP 2013 selected records management functions are available. However, these capabilities are generally not used by users.	limits. • "Documents without ownership": For example, "orphaned" SharePoint sites and retaining business contacts that no longer operate. After a project has ended more documents than necessary are saved. Business owner leaves the company - "data cemetery". Technical Risks include: • Scalability (<??)for larger volumes of documents • Migration of documents as part of the 3 year Microsoft Update cycle=> expenses may be incurred (especially if additional functions have been programmed) • Elaborate migration, if the company has no set standards (e.g. 500 different SharePoint sites)

4.4.7.2 Challenges of Information Governance

The company should establish clear guidelines for what information and which documents SharePoint may be used for. Typical usage scenarios for SharePoint include the filing of project documentation and the creation of intranet sites for corporate initiatives.

For use in the field of document management, or for the development of applications (e.g. for departments and clearly defined fields of application), a review should be carried out for each project as to whether or not SharePoint is useful from the perspective of IT strategy and business benefits.

Checklist	Information Governance SharePoint
Business and IT Owner • **A SharePoint governance model needs to be developed by the company**	• How are business sites governed? Is there a business owner for each site? • How can SharePoint sites be categorised across the enterprise? For example, a company may choose to use the categories of (a) temporary document storage (projects), (b) permanent information services, (c) development of applications. • How can business and IT determine which use will be implemented for a planned project (Risk: Business leads a shadow IT)? • SharePoint Governance Board: What additional third-party applications will be used to enhance functions? Do these features affect document retention and migration?
Retention periods SharePoint RM functions	• Has the company chosen which SharePoint sites the SP-records management function ("records center") will be applied to? Usually an add-on is needed to fulfill the requirements. Out-of-the-box functionality of SP is not sufficient.
Approvals in SharePoint	• Is the need for approval processes of certain application fields noted in SharePoint? • Are there restrictions on the technical implementation (e.g. Pharma) or digital signatures are necessary? • Is the audit trail maintained even after migration?
New SharePoint software versions	Every three years Microsoft introduces a new version of Sharepoint. How is the migration between versions managed by the company?

4.4.8 Social Media

External social media services

Opportunities	Risks
• Companies and employees are present on the internet **• networking with customers and suppliers** **• companies "keep up with the times" - Social media monitoring Social Media building corporate** **• to improve employee communications. Social media and collaboration tools are growing together**	• Communication of confidential corporate information • Social hacking - data can be obtained and used by external attackers • Reputational risk: scandals, nude pictures, etc.

Checklist	Information Governance of Social Media
Detection of Activities / Records Mgt.	• Who is responsible for the various social media and chat systems? • Who maintains an overview of the applications, application runtime, and retention period?
Policy:	• What is allowed? Designation of the company name and job title in the profile (XING, LinkedIn, Facebook). • What is not allowed? • Communication of confidential corporate information • Reputational risks: scandals nude pictures etc. • How can grey areas be regulated? • sharing News / current Location: "I am at the conference and we will provide a new product .." • o Risk: Social hacking - data can be used by external attackers (Ms X is on vacation - they wanted to send me a file)
Training	• How do employees, through training and guidelines, deal with social media and present the company?

4.4.9 Cloud Applications

The use of cloud solutions in the enterprise can be divided into the following scenarios:

4.4.9.1 Data storage in the cloud (e.g. Dropbox)

Use of storage services for example Dropbox.

Cloud Storage

Opportunities	Risks
• Employees may at any time and from anywhere in access data **• Data can be edited on mobile and tablet devices** **• Data can be securely exchanged with external partners and customers (if cloud service offers this)**	• Unauthorised use: how can one check whether employees unknowingly save critical private data private, e.g. for use on iPad? • Data in the cloud is not deleted (staff have no time or change companies, changing providers) • Filing and storage of business-critical data constitutes a security hazard • Deletion of the data must be performed within the company and in the cloud • Risk of data loss if data is not archived internally in addition to the cloud

Checklist	Information Governance
Management decisions	• Which cloud services are used officially (Gmail, Microsoft Azure)?
Business and IT Owner	• Who is the owner of the cloud application? • What are the responsibilities and processes of internal IT and the IT cloud provider? • How can the company manage multiple cloud providers?
Cloud	• Data protection • Data location management and legal regulations • Risk of default of the cloud service • Risk of insolvency or acquisition of

Checklist	Information Governance
	the cloud provider
Interfaces	• The question is raised as to whether the respective cloud software provider may offer an appropriate interface.
Backup	• In the case of failure of the cloud service, can the company access the data? If a backup of the data exists within the enterprise can functions be executed?
Archiving	• Is the process of archiving data and documents defined? Is date archived in the Cloud (leads to long-term contracts and dependencies) or is it transferred to the corporate archives?

4.4.9.2 Cloud-Based Hosting Solutions (e.g. Amazon)

Companies use select cloud applications for hosting in an effort to, for example, better integrate field staff.

Information Governance Challenges:

• The cloud platform must comply with standards

• Governance and management of the content must be ensured and enforced.

• Availability of data ownership information

• What happens at the end of the contract; who owns the data?

4.4.9.3 Cloud-based Solutions for Specific Industries (e.g. Veeva)

Some sectors have established suppliers with finite services. It is, for example, in the pharmaceutical industry usual for marketing agencies to review documents found in active cloud-based systems.

Information Governance Challenges:

•If business stakeholders directly communicate with external providers, there is a risk that IT-governance will be neglected.

4.4.10 Apps for Mobile Use

4.4.10.1 Use of Commercial Apps

Scenario: a company must decide on which mobile applications should be utilised by certain employee groups, e.g. Sales.

Information Governance Challenges:

• Corporate data should officially be processed by App A , however, an employee has App B privately installed, which is able to forward data to external services.

• Advantage: certain applications can delete and distribute documents (marketing presentations) to terminals. In this "best case" scenario employees are always supplied with the latest information.

• Challenges: Communication channels through apps in addition to e-mail must now be managed.

4.4.10.2 Development Corporate Apps

Scenario: A company develops its own app for mobile devices.

• The business / information-owner must manage both Intranet applications and mobile applications and ensure the current security requirements are met.

4.4.11 Tools to Manage an Enterprise-wide Retention Schedule or File Plan

Several vendors offer tools (ECM) to manage enterprise-wide retention schedules for filing. Companies that do not use these tools, use self-created databases / spreadsheets to achieve these functions. Typical features include:

• Figures of the taxonomy of the organisation, such as processes and document types (record series) and assignment of retention periods and trigger information

• Management of sources / references in accordance to the relevant legislation and industry standards. Some providers offer periodic updates of information, such as which laws have changed

• Automated Transfer of retention periods and trigger information to the document management systems and archive applications

• Automated Transfer of Legal Holds

Example:

Tools for managing storage plans / Archive plans

Prospects	Risks
• The vision of a fully networked and automated control of the retention period is an ideal vision, which is rarely encountered in everyday business. Usually ECM systems are doing a poor functional integration of metadata from retention schedules (correctly applying lifecycle attributes like retention periods and triggers).	• The introduction of a tool requires that personnel within the company (or external) are involved in the process. For many companies, such tools do not exist or have been dismantled. • More important than the tool is the knowledge of records management and the respective industry

4.4.12 Electronic Invoicing

The process of e-invoicing, the legal assessment, and the distinction between commercial law office, invoicing, and signature archives were described in detail in the Best Practice Guide 2nd edition (chap. XV.). At this point, little has changed. One finds that these processes are still too complicated and has to assume, from the changes in the law of neighbouring states, that this type of accounting hedge belongs to in past. Nevertheless, there have been repeated attempts to resurrect projects, the last of which is called "ZUGFeRD".

In Germany, anew data standard for electronic invoices was published in June 2014. E-invoices in the format "ZUGFeRD" are digital documents (in PDF / A format) with embedded invoice data in machine-readable form (XML). Here it should be mentioned that such standards (e.g. As the INVOICE message in EDIFACT standard) have existed for decades. In Germany there have been, since 2013, two options for sending an e-bill, for example, e-mail: (a) PDF invoice is provided with a digital signature, or (b) PDF invoice does not contain a digital signature, but the receiver provides through an in-house control procedures authenticity, integrity, and legibility of the invoices safely. The receiver thus has a reliable audit trail between performance and accounting.

The German format "ZUGFeRD" supports the recipient in automating the audit. The latter is likely to provide advertised, in today's legal situation, as the only (laudable) way to introduce an automated process.

In Switzerland, a digital signature in the PDF invoice is imperative. But also, in Switzerland, the format "ZUGFeRD" can be used to optimise the audit.

The format PDF/A-3 must be used, since attachments (the invoice data in XML format) can be embedded. The archiving system must archive and process the XML metadata the PDF document.

4.5 Case Study: E-Discovery

4.5.1 The Cera-Break episode

To introduce the topic of e-discovery is a short story, which is fictitious but feasible:

The Swiss company "CeraBreak" specialises in the production of ceramic brake pads and is a supplier of the automotive industry, mainly in the field of sports car production. "CeraBreak" is one of three leading companies and is very successful in this area. The CEO of the company receives post from the Competition Commission (Comco). Comco is investigating allegations of unfair price fixing by automotive suppliers. The Competition Commission requires that CeraBreak secures and hands over all physical and electronic documents which have relevance to such potential price-fixing in the last 10 years. The Competition Commission explains in a letter, in detail, the consequences of non-cooperative behaviour or insufficient / incomplete disclosure of relevant data. In addition, the Competition Commission sets the date for the first meeting with CeraBreak.

The CEO contacted the Director of Legal Affairs with the request to investigate these allegations promptly and to hand over all documents requested by the Competition Commission. The Director of Legal Affairs consults the filing plan of the company, which systematically lists the records of the company and their retention periods. He decides to begin his investigation with the sales figures and requests from the head of sales all sales figures from the last 10 years. The sales manager elicits all the reports for the past 10 years present in the ERP system and delivers it to the General Counsel. The General Counsel presents the reports the sales figures to the CEO. It quickly becomes clear that the relevant documents are not likely to be found in these reports. The relevant documents are most likely to be found in the electronic communication system, such as e-mails. In addition, it can be assumed that potentially every employee in the sales department (about 8 people) could have made arrangements to fix prices or have been involved in such action. The CEO and the General Counsel decide to task the external law firm "iDisco" with the investigation, since they both imagine the company is in the middle of an eDiscovery case. As part of the outsourcing strategy, the company "CeraBreak" closed a well-defined agreement on e-discovery services with “iDisco” three years ago.

The law firm "iDisco" requires an e-Discovery project leader to head the e-Discovery Response Team (EDRT) for this e-discovery case. The experienced project leader provides an overview of the possible data that must be examined. He realises that the employees of the sales department are the "data custodians" of the relevant information. For the last 10 years the following data from the sales department and its personnel is required: all present company e-mails, all records of telephone conversations (e.g. call records.), data on mobile phones and documents stored on personal and group drives. The project manager makes it clear that every stone must be turned over to find potentially relevant information. He points out that other suppliers are also being examined and possible price agreements between CeraBreak and another company might be discovered in the other company’s records.

The Head of IT receives from the Head of Human Resources a complete list of all employees in the sales department from the last 10 years including their personnel (or personal) numbers. The central system for identity management "MyDentity" manages user data, such as e-mail addresses or Windows login names of all employees - current and historical. The operation of IT can use the system "MyDentity" to create a complete, consistent, and reliable list of all employee (also leaked) system identities. The list is used as a basis for finding the relevant data in the data sources. The reports from the central bi-temporal user authorization system "Role IT" outwit all IT systems used by employees. This allows the EDRT to use the Custodian Data Map to create a full and complete overview of the data sources used by the individual employees during the period in question. The email archive "ArchiveMe" was introduced six years ago and contains all e-mails of the last six years. Backups of e-mail servers before the introduction of the e-mail archive no longer exist. The e-mail data on these old backup tapes were migrated to the archive when ArchiveMe was first introduced. In addition, all PST files were migrated to the e-mail archive and "PST archiving" was rendered impossible. But now it is possible to access the mail archive its data . Although this process was expensive, the head of IT seven years ago was able to convince the management (GL) to conform to this requirement. Data on personal drives exists only for active employees; 32 days after they leave the company, the personal drives former employees are automatically deleted. Operational backup tapes do not exist for the shared network drives, as the infrastructure has a sophisticated failover and is operated at two locations. The same is true for group drives.

After a week of intensive e-Discovery research the Project Manager of GL submits a well-thought-out plan including deadlines and the costs of collecting, processing, classifying, and producing data. The largest cost arises in regards to the emails. Almost 2 million emails must be extracted from the archive, which will take roughly 20 days. The mobile e-discovery platform "mobile MyDisco" can upload, index and search 300,000 emails per day. In seven days all emails should be uploaded and the first search can begin. The EDRT expects a reduction of the data by a factor of 100.

If each sales employee sends an average of 2,000 emails per month the following calculation 10 years * 12 months * 8 employees * 2,000 emails reveals that a total of 1,920,000 emails were sent during the years in question

That leaves approximately 20,000 e-mails to be reviewed (1st Level Review) by five trained lawyers per day. For those staff members an additional 10 days is added to the total time and after 37 days any sign of price fixing ("smoking gun") should have been found. The CEO is satisfied with the process and he informs the Competition Commission on the procedure and the timetable. The Competition Commission is in contact with the Federal Cartel

Office in Germany and the Federal Competition Authority in Austria, which are investigating the same allegations against two other competitors of CeraBreak in their countries.

After 40 days of concentrated work of EDRT together with the IT and the legal department striking proof exists. In a production run, the relevant emails and sales documents are completed and then transmitted to the Competition Commission. Six weeks after the Competition Commission first request all relevant documents have arrived. The documents in the Competition Commission's possession show that both competitors were involved in price agreements. However, these companies have yet to submit any documents and have asked authorities for a lengthy extension. After 4 months, the fellow competitors send their relevant documents to the federal cartel office in Germany. This is when sighting common ground that the already known by the Competition Commission E-mail is not present in the documentation (but must be presented) and have also been more massive and systematic price-fixing agreements between the two competitors (via email).

A good reviewer can browse and evaluate approximately 400 pages per day. Twenty thousand e-mails, with 5 reviewers and an average review performance of 400 pages/day, will require approximately 10 days for the review.

This episode describes the ease with which a possible E Discovery case may arise and is described as a "best case" scenario. He is in the management of the E-Discovery-Falls CeraBreak optimal for the company. This case is a clear example, which demonstrates a company's need to address and determine a procedure for the procurement of requested data.

4.5.2 Introduction

E-Discovery has become, in the last few years, increasingly important to large enterprises and is regularly employed in entire departments. But smaller and medium-sized companies are increasingly confronted with e-discovery issues and do not know how to cope. The term e-discovery is less than 10 years old. The Electronic Discovery concept was created in December 2006 as a result of the revision of the US American Civil Procedure (FRCP), in which the disclosure of "Electronically Stored Information" (now with ESI abbreviated) is discussed and the first use of the term Electronic Discovery or as shorthand "e-discovery" was revealed. The revision followed various legal disputes involving electronic data and its disclosure. One of the most famous cases was Zubulake v. UBS Warburg LLC, 229 FRD 422, 437 (S.D.N.Y. 2004). The term e-discovery is now used worldwide and not just in US law. In this chapter, in addition to the classical definition of e-discovery by US law, the general disclosure of electronic data in legal cases or similar incidents (proof template) is addressed. Such incidents, for example, include the request for the disclosure of information to a regulatory or investigative authority. It may be necessary, under certain circumstances, to disclose electronic company data that relates to the incident. It is also possible that a company may be indirectly obliged to disclose electronic data, without being a primary party in the proceedings, but instead a witness.

In eDiscovery, it is irrelevant whether such data is stored in an archive, magnetic backup tapes, or whether it is located in operational systems. While electronic data is, for the most part, well indexed in archives for quick searches and extraction of evidence, the search and extraction of data from operational systems is a major challenge. In some legal systems, the search and extraction of data may be dismissed if the cost of disclosure of electronic data is. However it should be assumed that all electronic data existing in a company must be disclosed, regardless of their ease of access.

4.5.3 Who should read this chapter?

The following short self-assessment enables readers to decide whether the chapter on E-discovery is of interest to them:

- Is the company (or subsidiary of the company) under US jurisdiction?
- Is the company (or subsidiary of the company) under EU jurisdiction?
- Does the business operate in a regulated industry, such as the financial sector, energy, or telecommunications industry?
- Does / did the business possess electronic data that is used for litigation or similar subjects and was the cost of

the disclosure high or was the authenticity of the disclosed data doubted or denied?
- Were penalties or sanctions ever imposed on the company due to the inadequate or insufficient disclosure of electronic data?

If "yes" was the answer to any one of these questions then this section should be read.

4.5.4 Why is e-discovery important?

Insufficient e-discovery can have severe and far-reaching consequences. It can be expected that such consequences will increase in severity in the future. Here is a list (not extensive) of possible consequences:
- Sanctions and penalties (the EU General Data Protection Regulation has proposed a dramatic punishment of "a fine of up to 100,000,000 EUR or 5% of the annual worldwide turnover in the case of an enterprise, whichever is greater").
- Penalties in accordance with US law which are explicitly provided for in the Federal Rules of Civil Procedure.
- Evidence and proof of security legal case: One of the biggest risks associated with eDiscovery cases is the incomplete nature of disclosed information. That is, the absence of a relevant document. The opposition can use this absence of the document at the hearing. It is possible the authenticity and integrity of the data collected will be challenged in court as it is no longer possible to be sure where documents originated, how they were obtained, and how they were processed.
- "Leniency" for voluntary disclosure (unfair collusion, manipulation, cartels, etc.). It is of fundamental importance that eDiscovery is efficient and fast. The party under suspicion may benefit from voluntary disclosure by receiving "leniency" and possibly reduced (monetary) penalties. Corresponding facts and evidence for such voluntary disclosure must be collected, searched, viewed, evaluated, and produced.
- Mitigation in good co-operation: a public authority may take into consideration the will of cooperation and the

quality of the investigation when assessing the penalty. There is no guarantee of leniency and payment for punitive reductions is almost never published. Reports of authorities allow appropriate conclusions on investigations[64]: "The investigation of FINMA was significantly supported by the thoroughness of the internal investigation of the bank".

4.5.5 Reasons for Submission

The disclosure of electronic data may be necessary in one of the following instances (the list is not extensive):

- Court case
- Internal investigation by compliance / internal audit
- Whistleblowing case
- Regulatory authorities requesting information
- External investigation by regulatory authority (or an external auditor who was commissioned by a regulatory authority)
- Information requested by an individual person (e.g. Subject access request in the UK and now also in the EU General Data Protection Regulation)
- Labour law offenses, such as fraud or sexual harassment
- E-Discovery by American Civil Procedure (Federal Rules of Civil Procedure (FRCP)).

In this chapter, the term e-discovery is more generally used more than the "Discovery of ESI", an American Civil Procedure that is covered explicitly in the chapter "American eDiscovery".

---

[4] 6: See, also, the report of the FINMA for Currency manipulation (page 7, second paragraph):

4.5.6 eDiscovery Reference Model

Intertwined with eDiscovery is the eDiscovery Reference Model (EDRM), which proposes a standardised procedure in five phases:

1. "Identification" includes finding relevant data for the present case. This includes, in particular, the identification of potential data sources such as IT systems or personal information shelves of affected employees (custodians). "Identification" can also be regarded as a planning phase in which, not only have the data sources been identified, but also the expenses (costs and schedules) for the search and extraction from the source. As a result of "identification" there is a collection (discovery) / Preservation plan for the subsequent phases. US eDiscovery uses the "meet-and-confer"- Meeting in which the parties agree on the scope of data disclosure at the very beginning of the process. A robust discovery plan is a central component of such meetings. Even without this meeting, it makes sense to plan for data disclosure before it is performed.

2. The "Collection" or "Preservation" of data from identified data sources is the next phase. The search and extraction (export) of data performed directly from the data source through appropriately provided functions and authorised personnel (e.g. archive system) or the IT data steward who is responsible for obtaining the data. The IT Data Steward is, in many cases, a person with administrative authority over data. Many operational systems lack the appropriate search / export functions of an archive system. For example, the procurement of an e-mail from an electronic mailbox of an employee an order addressed to the administrator of the mail server. In "Preservation" data is not obtained, but protected from changes including deletion. For an archive, the disposal hold function is used (in-place Preservation), provided that they meet the minimum requirements for such a function (see also MoReq 2, Ref 5.1.34 cf ("MoReq2 MODEL FOR THE REQUIREMENTS FOR ELECTRONIC RECORDS"). If the data source does not have a disposal hold function the procurement of data is followed by safe keeping to perform Preservation)

3. “Processing” the data involved the examining of data for important information (“search term responsive documents”) and provides information for the review. For this, eDiscovery software is generally used as it is specialised in providing search functions (searches based on taxonomy, Fuzzy Search, predictive coding, etc.). Of course, processing is only relevant if the collected amount of data cannot be manually screened and spotted by hand. If only a dozen documents are required then specialised eDiscovery software is not necessary. These documents can also be viewed and assessed directly. eDiscovery is the most cost-efficient and fastest method for separating all potentially relevant documents from non-relevant information.
4. In “Review”, the data provided by Processing will be viewed and assessed. What remains are the relevant documents concerning the case. Even specialised eDiscovery software can be used to support the Review. During the review, the documents are reviewed (tagging) and possibly also blacked out (redact). The review classifies documents in predefined groups as “relevant to the case”, for example “private’ or “contains a mystery” (a legal, such as medical, banking, attorney-client privilege or even a trade secret). The review is an important tool in the review. The review will carry out by a specialised legal person and can be carried out in several stages for cost reasons (for example 1. Review is conducted by lawyers with expert statements, 2. Review by partners of a law firm with much less Documents from the 1st Review). The blackening of information in documents is carried out before “Production” and prevents the disclosure of protected information such as bank customer data, patient information, etc. The final stage is “production”, in which data is prepared for handover. It may be necessary under certain circumstances to convert document formats as defined by the other parties (or even the counterparty). . The possible formats are “original format”, “the origin of similar format” (such as PDF), “paper like format” (image file such as TIFF) or paper format (this format is not required, because it is neither electronic nor searchable).

During these five stages complete documentation of the procurement and processing of data is essential. These stages form the chain of custody. Each step is carefully documented in writing so that it is always possible to trace who did what and when with the data. The audit trails of good e-Discovery software should ensure complete documentation. In contrast, all manual performed outside of the software must be documented completely and separately. This poses a big administrative challenge as such manual documentation is often prone to errors.

The EDRM has become the de-facto industry standard. All eDiscovery consultants and manufacturers of software are a member of this coalition.

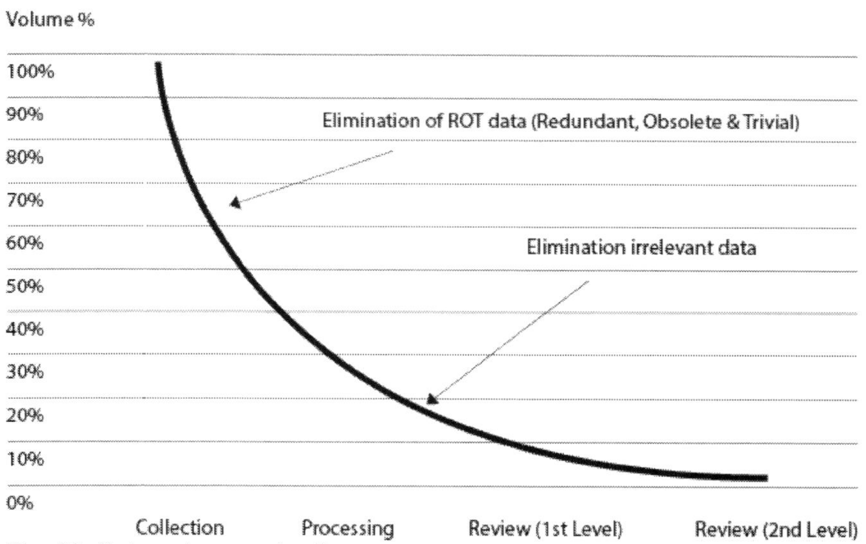

Fig. 23: Data volume reduction

4.5.7 Problem areas

The biggest challenges in eDiscovery stem from the identification and procurement (collection) of unstructured data in archives and operational systems. In the figure below, the process stages indicated by the EDRM are located on the vertical axis and the data type on the horizontal. The most important and thus the primary focus of the chapter on eDiscovery are shown in red on the graphic below. This illustration is explicitly not a legal assessment / approach but instead describes the best practices according to experience and corresponding do's and don'ts listed.

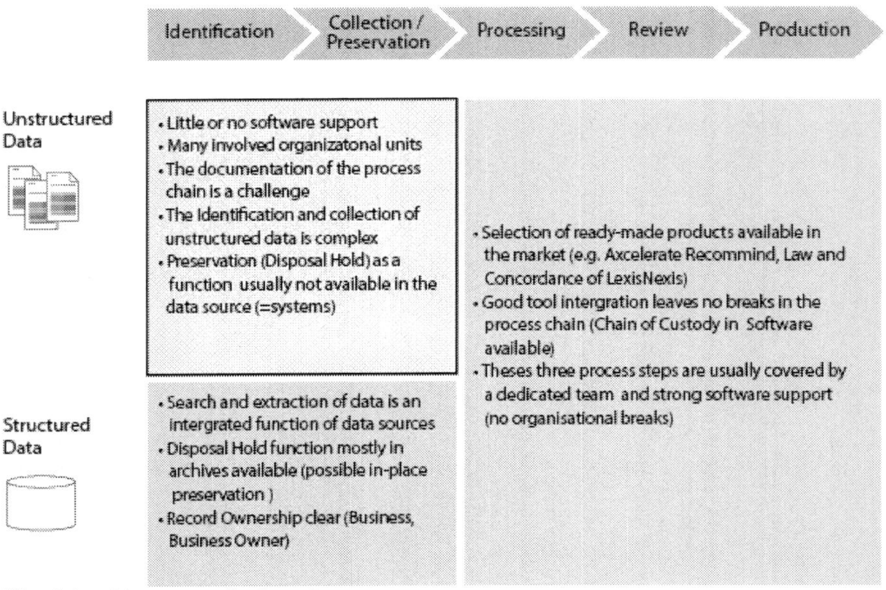

Fig. 24: eDiscovery hotspots

Unstructured data content is cannot classified, aggregated, or used automatically. Unstructured data includes semi-structured data such as e-mail, as their contents are unstructured. Structured data includes transport and details such as sender, recipient, date, and subject. Estimates suggest that 75% of all data is unstructured.

4.5.8 Long-term backup: Pandora's Box

Magnetic backup tapes have a very high storage density and are more cost-effective compared to disk drives. Magnetic backup-tapes (or, more generally, replacement backups) should not be used as an operational disaster recovery solution for data loss.

Backup tapes retained for periods longer than one year are a clear indication of a hidden archive system.

In particular, backups with a retention period of several years (in some cases decades) in dedicated physical archives do not maintain the original purpose of data recovery in the case of unexpected loss, but rather correspond to an archive without possessing the necessary characteristics of an archive (see table below).

Backups with a long-term storage (greater than 1 year) might appear at first glance to be a cost effective solution for the "archiving" of data. Disk storage is cheap as there are no costly maintenance costs for an archive solution. But such backup storage systems pose massive risks for both potential access, i.e. the restoration of data from a backup (collection), and the legal hold (preservation).

Restoring data requires not only physical infrastructure such as readers for stocked data formats but also software infrastructure for accessing data. Should the stored backup data be encrypted for security reasons, it is then necessary to have the corresponding key and hardware for decryption.

The risks are much greater when a legal hold is active. One can also use backup infrastructure designed for efficiency and cost. That is to say, data that belongs together can, in the case of backups, be separated by being put on different tapes.

The following table shows the functions of an archive on a backup at an abstract level.

Function	Archive	Backup
Security (access, audit trails, backup & recovery)	Yes	Limited, the loss of backups is irreversible
Disposal hold	Yes	No, cannot be implemented at the level of a record
Indexing, metadata and keywords Verzeichnung	Yes	No, within the backup content there is no metadata (at best, a catalogue), no index, and no classification
Format and presentability of records	Yes	No
Search	Yes	No, users cannot browse backups

Function	Archive	Backup
Rendering & readability	Yes	Very limited: for the restoration of stored data sometimes specialised software needed
Disposal at the record level	Yes	No, only an entire backup can be destroyed, not non-specific records within the backup
High integrity and probative value	Yes	No, correct operation of long-term backup tapes cannot be guaranteed; documentation of the process chain must be manually ensured
Active management of data and system	Yes	No, the data on the backups and the backups themselves are not managed

4.5.9 Solutions

For existing long-term backups, questions arise as to whether the destruction of expired backups is possible and how to them destroyed successfully. In an ideal scenario of the destruction of such backups there is no need for action. However, out dated backups that cannot be destroyed easily, may exist and must be immediately addressed. Differentiating outdated data is extremely dangerous and ineffective. In the case of expired long-term backups, archiving of relevant data is a prerequisite for the destruction of these backups. The archiving or destruction of large number of expired backups can quickly turn into a large complex task that be addressed with thorough advance planning and budgeting.

4.5.10 identification of relevant information

Identifying the relevant information for an eDiscovery case is primarily, about isolating the business data and documents in the present case and, secondly, determining data sources.

The identification of data and documents relevant to the case is often called “scoping” (the scope). The following three areas are of importance:

1. The key players and persons with relevant information on the case (data custodians): Who are the people involved in the case? Which people have relevant information? Information on the organisational structure during the defined period (for example valid organisational charts) can be valuable sources of information
2. Period: Every case should have a start and end data and the events should correlate to the period
3. The relevant information (documents and data): This pertains to the question of which documents and data are relevant. In a case regarding price fixing, the relevant information can most likely be found in the communication (e-mail, phone calls, instant messaging) and personal storage. In a fraud case relevant information would be found within bank statements and statements of account voters. The first step is to determine what information is relevant not where (in which system) it is stored.

The methodology for the identification of data depends on the kind of case. Interviews with key players and data custodians performed by the investigator can prove to be a very effective approach. The use of a structured questionnaire which requests the potential types of data for varying business transactions is possible. In a highly confidential investigation, the persons concerned must not be contacted. In this case, the identification of relevant information will be much more difficult as the directly concerned may not provide any information.

To determine the data sources containing the relevant information, a list of data (the data map) can be helpful. This should serve as a generic catalogue as well as describe the relevant records of a business unit. In addition, a list describing the systems in which the data is stored in detail would also prove useful.

4.5.11 The Bi-temporal User Permission System (User Entitlement System) and the bi-temporal Identity Management System

The bi-temporal User authorisation system (user entitlement system) manages and documents the permissions of employees for the IT systems of the company. Whenever possible, a centralised user authentication system should be used as it administers the rights of all IT systems (applications and resources) and historicising (storing?) the permissions in future (i.e. bi-temporal) stores. The authentication, authorization, and access control of an application are often not clearly separated. The bi-temporal user authorization system manages the authorizations of employees and outputs or provides this data to the relevant IT systems. If all access to managed IT systems uses the bi-temporal user privilege system, the user authorization system can provide information about which employees, over what period, to which IT systems, and with which rights were granted access.

The bi-temporal identity management system manages and documents the user data, the individuals associated in the system. The identity management system consolidates the various login credentials (i.e. accounts) of a person (e.g. email address, account for the operating system, instant messaging nick names, login for ERP applications, etc.). A person can have multiple accounts when usually only one account per application is assigned to each person. In an identity management system, a person is uniquely identifiable (for example, through a unique personal number / employee number) and thus the person at some point is associated with accounts for applications. Applications even manage the accounts and related information, but not the people. Access must be managed bi-temporally. That is, data regarding granted access to persons in the identity management system must be stored and retrievable at any time. Without a bi-temporal identity management system it would, for example, be difficult to identify the correct e-mail address of any employee at a given time.

4.5.12 Data Collection

Having identified what data in which application (data source) is relevant, it must then be located and extracted. Corresponding order for the search and extraction of relevant data are granted by the IT data stewards and / or the custodians who are then directly instructed to the gather the data (custodian self-collection).

Direct orders addressed to a custodian can be very efficient or possibly the only way, in certain circumstances, to gain access to the relevant documents. Physical paper documents are what the custodians can obtain in this manner.

Each data extraction should always include a description of the data to be produced (delivery manifest). The delivery manifesto provides, among other things, the weight of evidence in a legal case. As a benchmark for the quality of a delivery manifest the following criteria should be met:

- Reproducibility of results: Using the information from the order book and delivery manifesto, can data be reproduced at any time (repeatability after the search and extraction)?
- Chain of custody: Which person (who) has done what with the data and at what date and time?
- For information security, the integrity and confidentiality of data must be guaranteed. Note: For the authenticity of data, the IT data steward or the data source itself is responsible

4.5.13 The Needle in the Haystack

Finding the potentially relevant documents concerning a specific case is one of the most important features of eDiscovery. Search engines play a central role and are already installed in many IT systems. In addition, searches are applied to several stages in the eDiscovery process. Firstly, the required data can be searched for in the source systems thus reducing the amount of documents to be collected substantially. Searches can be as simple as “Find all documents from Custodian A in the period XY” or possibly require keywords or full text, or it may a combination of the two such as "Find all documents from Custodian A in the period XY, in which the term, ‘kickback' or ‘complacency' occurs ". In further data processing, data is filtered by very specialised search engines and algorithms. This method, the conceptual search, taxonomy-based search, and clustering and categorization allow for predictive coding. Predictive coding is not a search engine or algorithm, but a learning function that can generalise the information and decisions of individuals and then applies what it learns to a larger set of documents.

Key factors in the field of search for eDiscovery include the search time and quality of the search for relevant documents. The quality of the search always carries dimension of risk and cost. The following comments are intended to illustrate this. The recall ratio (hit rate) and the precision ratio (accuracy) determine the quality of the search. The recall ratio measures the ability of a search result listing all existing relevant documents. The precision ratio measures the ratio of relevant documents in a search result to the amount of total number of documents listed. Recall and precision ratios arise as follows:

$$Recall, R = \frac{Number\ of\ relevant\ documents\ in\ the\ search\ results}{Number\ of\ relevant\ documents\ in\ the\ sample\ population}$$

$$Precision, P = \frac{Number\ of\ relevant\ documents\ in\ the\ search\ results}{Number\ of\ documents\ in\ the\ search\ result}$$

An example will illustrate the recall and precision ratio. A set of data has 36 documents of which 20 are relevant. 12 documents were found in a search of which 8 are relevant and 4 not. The recall and precision ratios are as follows:
Recall = 8/20 = 0.4
Precision = 8/12 ≈ 0.67

The search result made 4 false positive results and 12 false negatives (of the 20 relevant documents only 8 were found to actually be relevant while 12 were not):

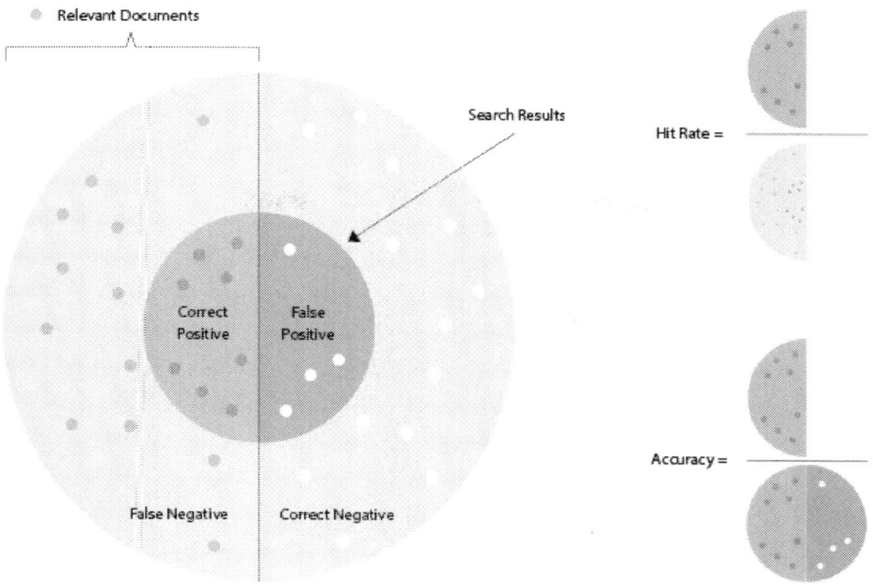

Fig. 25: Hit rate

Ideally, both the highest possible recall ratio as well as high precision are achieved in a search. Of course, search engines are not perfect. A low recall ratio increases the risk that the "smoking gun" cannot be found and the case jeopardised. A low precision ratio causes the cost of processing and reviewing documents to rise and impacts the application of data privacy and employment laws. The quality of the search is of fundamental importance in eDiscovery and is influenced by many factors.

In addition to the full-text, metadata is also indexed by almost all search engines. The indexing and search for metadata are far less problematic as the integrity of the metadata index is influenced by very few factors. A full-text index is almost never complete. The reasons for this are very diverse, ranging from the abortion of indexing for large documents, encrypted documents, to unsupported document formats.

Apart from the quality of the engine and the comprehensiveness of the index, the stability and integrity of keywords are important. Terms can change over time (the Swiss financial market supervisory authority FINMA was previously known as SFBC) or different terms or spellings may have the same use.

Thus it is extremely important in eDiscovery that the methods (and any possible shortcomings) a search engine uses (including the index) are known before it is used. Unknown, inadequate, or even incorrect use of a search engine (including the index) can become a high-level risk because the recall of the applied search is poor and the smoking gun is not found quickly.

4.5.14 Process Organisation

eDiscovery is not a technology but a process involving well-trained employees, who use specialised software to support their activities. An eDiscovery event is always handled by an interdisciplinary team; the eDiscovery Response Team (EDRT). A typical eDiscovery response team is comprised of the following professionals with specific functions:

- Internal lawyer of the legal department to supervise the case
- External lawyer (unless an external firm is commissioned by the enterprise)
- IT Specialists
- Records Manager
- HR staff
- IT Security officer (IT security)
- Data protection officer
- eDiscovery expert and/or eDiscovery vender
- eDiscovery project manager
- Head of departments ("line of business", LOB executives)

An eDiscovery case must be considered as a project. It is the task of the eDiscovery response team to assume project management of the present case and all costs incurred. The eDiscovery project manager (or eDiscovery case manager) is responsible for the efficient, effective, and low risk settlement of the case. In particular, an ad hoc team (see below) provides an experienced eDiscovery project manager for the necessary structure and organisation. Not having an eDiscovery response team is not an option!

4.5.15 Process Documentation

Although the EDRM consortium presents the proposed process phases as a basis for discussion, these phases should be assumed to be fixed in the documentation and may not be changed without a compelling reason. The EDRM framework is not the only possible way to tackle an eDiscovery case but it provides a good structure for the understanding and approach from start to finish.

It is important to compile interdisciplinary teams with clear structures and role descriptions for the various phases for the important activities and responsibilities in eDiscovery.

The chain of custody ensures the value of evidence data in an eDiscovery case. Basically: The higher the proportion of manually handled data, the more demanding the documentation needed by the chain of custody. The documentation should include the following information in each phase:

- Where is the data stored?
- Who has access to the data?
- What was done with the data?
- All transfers of data from a sender to a recipient (for example, from the IT data steward to the eDiscovery team, from the eDiscovery team to the external attorney's office, etc.)
- All problems / exceptions and their treatment
- All necessary permits, such as who granted access to the data, who approved the transfer of data (outbound transfer, transfer from one jurisdiction to another, transfer by a legal person to another)

Evaluating the permitted documentation is a central task of eDiscovery response teams. It involves both the licenses for accessing data and the data source itself. Furthermore, the transfer of data must be carefully planned and permits documented. Trans-border data transfers during eDiscovery are critical, particularly in transfers from Europe to the United States. Existing European data protection directives are not completely compatible with eDiscovery law in the US (Hartmann, n.d.)

The provision of appropriate work equipment, such as templates, checklists, and software is a logical consequence of the documentation process. In addition, dedicated checkpoints for quality control must be provided. These result, on one hand, from known process steps, or at steps which have caused problems in the past. Basically, problems in the process are always to be expected confronted at interfaces (either organisational or technical interfaces).

4.5.16 Legal Hold (Preservation)

As part of an eDiscovery action, the identified data must be protected from destruction. The offense and specified scope of preservation can be defined by an external party, for example a regulatory authority (i.e. Preservation Letter), or internally by an anticipation of a possible future eDiscovery cases. However, even in US eDiscovery cases, the obligation of the protection of data from possible destruction is not clearly established.

The Legal Hold process (see section 4.5.17) examines the execution of such a process in accordance with the type of case and the involvement of people directly affected, even if only through IT data stewards and IT systems. In a confidential internal investigation of suspected wrongdoing by individuals, this may of course not be possible. In in this instance, the preservation order is implemented by the eDiscovery team together with the IT data stewards (people with administrative control over data). In another eDiscovery case, the persons directly concerned must be contacted (i.e. Product Liability) and a dual action mounted. People directly affected {involved in the case} will receive written Legal Hold notices and the eDiscovery team, working with the IT data stewards, will prevent the destruction of data in the IT systems.

The implementation of IT systems begins with the identification of relevant data and data sources. Determining whether the IT systems (data sources) are identified is a test of the ability of the system to prevent data destruction. The system's built-in functions, relevant records prior to destruction, and possible implementation of a destruction stop must be protected. Generally, it is best to use adequate archiving systems with disposal hold functions available. MoReq2 contains the requirements for a system to include disposal-hold capabilities

The lack of Information Governance management regarding data disposal and the obligation to preserve data can quickly lead to the cessation of data destruction. Those who can destroy data, control it!

4.5.17 Legal Hold Process

The legal hold process starts with the kick-off (trigger) of an instruction to stop the destruction of data. As already mentioned in the introduction, the reasons for a trigger can be diverse and not always clearly identifiable. Identifying triggers and the impetus of the legal hold process is the responsibility of the Legal Department.

The rough sequence is as follows:

- Trigger: Written complaint, indictment, criminal charge, request by an authority, existing eDiscovery case
- Scope: Once the trigger is recognised, a destruction stop is necessary and the scope must be defined. Who are the people directly concerned (custodians)? What is the relevant period of time (from start date to end date) and which information is relevant? Defining the scope is the first important milestone of a legal hold process and requires the inclusion of an interdisciplinary eDiscovery team. The first call for a destruction stop is general in many cases (e.g. "any available information in connection with the development, production, and distribution of product XYZ"). It is necessary to define the scope as precisely as possible:
    - What is relevant? (When was the product XYZ developed, when was it produced, and how widely was it distributed?
    - Who is affected? Entire departments could be affected and therefore current and former organisation charts could be helpful. Which team developed the product XYZ? Who was involved in the production? Which team distributed the product?
    - What information is relevant? (Research results, construction plans, production plans, documentation, quality assurance, sales brochures,

sales numbers, correspondence such as email, etc.)

- Notification of the custodian (Hold Notice): In the case of a (legal) hold notice, the affected persons (custodians) are informed about the destruction stop and their duties described in detail: Which data must not be destroyed, instructions for the destruction stop (e.g. securing the data, transmitting the data to the eDiscovery team, etc.), acknowledgment of receipt of the notification, confirmation of implementation, and obligations to provide information about other relevant data which is not mentioned in the notice.
- Notification of the IT organisation: The eDiscovery team is notified together with the IT data stewards that a destruction stop is to be implemented on the identified data sources (identification of data sources, in-place disposal hold or collection of data).
- Enforcement and control: the aim is essentially to check that notifications have been received by the person concerned and instructions followed.
- Inventory, regular updates, and reminders: Many eDiscovery cases involving a destruction stop have a central register of all cases, persons concerned, and data sources available. The cases are to be reviewed periodically for accuracy and reminders are to be sent to the persons concerned.
- Lifting a legal hold: The aim must be to maintain a stop destruction order for as little time as possible. Each destruction stop lengthens the lifecycle of data and thus increases the cost and the risk for the next destruction stop. A central directory with open legal hold cases must be managed stringently.

To support the legal hold process, there is specialised software that automates the notification of persons concerned and provides a central directory. With a large number of custodians or cases, the use of such software is useful, as the management of work processes is more efficient and the process is already structured by the specialised software.

4.5.18 Summary

eDiscovery, Information Governance, and records management are all closely related. In an eDiscovery case, the Information Governance and records management processes of a company are put to the test. Detected shortcomings and problems in eDiscovery should flow directly to Information Governance and records management so that these problems can be resolved. This has been recognised by EDRM consortium that changed the name information management to Information Governance and created its own model (the Information Governance Reference Model, IGRM).

The earliest possible, complete, efficient, and effective retrieval of relevant information for eDiscovery cases while retaining the information's value throughout the process is of extraordinary importance to eDiscovery. This chapter provides an overview of pragmatic central points in the implementation of an eDiscovery case. The focus was not on the legal aspects, but on universal, best practices for problem areas, which can be applied to any legal area.

30160069R00094

Printed in Poland
by Amazon Fulfillment
Poland Sp. z o.o., Wrocław